A Perspective
on how our
Government
was Built
and Some Needed Changes

DARREL A NASH

ISBN 978-1-956001-15-0 (paperback)
ISBN 978-1-956001-16-7 (eBook)

Printed in the United States of America

Statue of James and Dolly Madison at Montpelier

Books by Darrel Nash

Book I, A Perspective on How Our Government
Was Built And Some Needed Changes

Book II, A Perspective on How Our Society Was
Built, Topics on Power in America

Some History and Reminiscences of the San Luis VAlley
Colorado, The United States in Microcosm

Contents

Foreword

I consider myself an informed citizen on matters of government. I have more than a casual interest in the US Constitution and related founding documents. A few years ago I read the entire compendium of the 85 Federalist Papers. These were written by proponents of ratifying the proposed Constitution that delegates of the existing states completed in 1787 and which came into force in 1789.

Over the years I have observed legislation and court decisions, especially the controversial ones relating to one or more elements of the Constitution to see how the proponents and opponents argue their validity. An organization called The Federalist Society publishes studies and advocacy positions claiming for themselves to be **the** interpreters of the founders' intent when the founders wrote The Federalist Papers and the US Constitution.

I have been puzzled by some of these cases and decisions and wondered if this was really the intent of the founders when the decisions are sometimes rather obviously not in the interest of US citizens or the nation.

So I embarked on a more thorough study of the Federalist Papers and related documents to help me, to the best of my ability, get some answers. This is a rather awesome task. I am not an expert in history, political science, or Constitutional law. There can be many interpretations besides mine. But most of the Federalist Papers are quite straightforward. Some of the arguments get a little obscure, but on the whole a person with a modest education and a fairly large amount of patience can get through them.

What I have found is a mixture. The founders purposely restricted participation in our government to upper class white males. But they did not—to use a current example—mandate that we are obligated to allow money to buy elections.

My first inclination, and I suspect it's the same for most readers of these documents, is to accept the reasoning and arguments presented. These are written by our founders, the most revered, dedicated and intelligent men. I had to push myself to read and think about several of their arguments to perceive what is said and separate this from the persons who wrote them. Here is what I found.

Read on.

Introduction

This book is presented in three separate parts. Although common threads run through all, each is a stand alone. Within each part are sections that also can be stand alone. In other words, this does not necessarily have to be read sequentially—the reader can go directly to a topic of interest. I hope that wherever you start, you are enticed into reading all of it.

Part One

We the People

CIVICS AND POLITICS

The US Constitution is a great document, looked to throughout the world as a model for how a government should relate to the citizens of a country. A primary—I would say—sacred provision or practice when persons are taking a high position in the US federal service is to take an oath that she or he do solemnly swear (or affirm) that she or he will faithfully execute [position], and will to the best of her or his ability, preserve, protect and defend the Constitution of the United States.

I do not remember if I took this oath in 1964 when I began my work for the federal government, but if I was asked to, I freely acceded to it. I would unhesitatingly do the same thing today.

But this in no way means that I accept this Constitution as the perfect legitimizing document for our country. Very significant changes to it are necessary to implement the objectives of the Constitutional convention that drafted it or the states that ratified it.

What were the objectives? *James Madison,* called the father of the Constitution writes in *Federalist Paper Number 45*;

"…We have heard of the impious doctrine of the Old World, that the people were made for kings, not kings for the people. Is the same doctrine not to be revived in the New [World] in a different shape—**that the solid happiness of the people is to be sacrificed to the laws of political institutions** of a different form? …It is too early for politicians to presume on our forgetting that **the public good, the real welfare of the great body of people, is the supreme object to be pursued, and that no form of government whatever has any other value than as it may be fitted for the attainment of this object.** Were the plan of the convention adverse to the public happiness, my voice would be, Reject the plan. Were the Union itself inconsistent with the public happiness, it would be Abolish the Union. **In like manner, as far as the sovereignty of the States cannot be reconciled to the happiness of the people, the voice of every good citizen must be, Let the former be sacrificed to the latter.** How far the sacrifice is necessary has been shown. How far the unsacrificed residue will be endangered, is the question before us."

To me, these are the most powerful words that have been written for why the Constitution was created.

If **the public good, the real welfare of the great body of people, is the supreme object to be pursued,** then the Constitution is seriously flawed. Is **the solid happiness of the people is to be sacrificed to the laws of political institutions** of a different form?

Our founders moved from the Articles of Confederation to the Constitution because the federal government had very little power and each individual State was not functioning very well. What we got was a Federation that gave some more, but limited, powers to the Federal Government.

When human rights activists and advocates, such as Abraham Lincoln and Rev. Dr. Martin Luther King described what our country is founded on, they cited the Declaration of Independence and the **Preamble** to the Constitution. Let's look at these items again, keeping in mind that the vast majority of us would now substitute "men and women" or "people" for "men". First the Declaration.

> "…We hold these truths to be self-evident, that all men are created equal; that they are endowed by their Creator with **certain unalienable rights; that among these are life, liberty, and the pursuit of happiness.** That to secure these rights, governments are instituted among men, **deriving their just powers from the consent of the governed;** that, whenever any form of government becomes destructive of these ends, it is the right of the people to alter or abolish it, and to institute a new government, laying its foundation on such principles, and **organizing its powers in such form, as to them shall seem most likely to affect their safety and happiness. …**"

Now the Constitution preamble.

> "**We the people of the United States**, in order to form a more perfect union, establish justice, insure domestic tranquility, provide for the common defense, promote the general welfare, and secure the blessings of liberty to ourselves and our posterity, do ordain and establish the Constitution of the United States of America."

I think that if we were naming this sentence today, we would call it a Vision Statement. This is what the authors envisioned for themselves and their posterity.* But I must acknowledge:

*The sequencing of preparing the body of the Constitution and the Preamble, unfortunately does not support the idea that the Constitution was written with the guidance of the Preamble. The Preamble was added after the Constitution was ratified. *Labunski, Ch. 9*

Note, "we the people..." Is this what we have?

Here are words from Abraham Lincoln and Dr. Martin Luther King.

[from Lincoln's Gettysburg Address, beginning and end]

"Four score and seven years ago (that would be 1776) our fathers brought forth, upon this continent, a new nation, conceived in liberty, and dedicated to the proposition that "all men are created equal."

Now we are engaged in a great civil war, testing whether that nation, or any nation so conceived, and so dedicated, can long endure."

"...that we here highly resolve these dead shall not have died in vain; that the nation, shall have a new birth of freedom, and that government **of** the people **by** the people **for** the people, shall not perish from the earth."

[King at the 1963, I have a Dream Speech]

"In a sense we have come to our nation's capital to cash a check. When the architects of our republic wrote the magnificent words of the Constitution and the declaration of Independence, they were signing a promissory note to which **every American** was to fall heir. This note was a promise **that all men would be guaranteed the inalienable rights of life, liberty, and the pursuit of happiness.**"

WE THE PEOPLE

I make a strong presumption that almost every adult, every school child, every teacher living in the United States, when they read the words, "we the people" think, yeah, that means me. But this is not what the Constitution provides. The Constitution went off track right away. It says it is a Constitution **for the people**, but from the beginning, it was and is a **States' rights** Constitution. The Tenth Amendment States, "The powers not delegated to the United States by the Constitution, nor prohibited by it to the States, are reserved to the States respectively, or to the people." If we are a **nation** of "we the people" should not the Federal Government delegate powers to the States? James Madison and Alexander Hamilton struggled with this—see below.

STATES' RIGHTS

The US Constitution grew out of the Articles of Confederation. Article Two of the Articles states, "Each state retains its sovereignty, freedom, and independence, and every power, jurisdiction, and right, which is not by this Confederation expressly delegated to the United States in Congress assembled." As we can already see, the beginning position of the Constitution was a modification of the Articles.

The Constitutional convention was called because many of the nation's leaders saw a lot of problems and weaknesses trying to function as a nation under the Articles. In *Federalist Paper Number 15, Alexander Hamilton* treats the reasons why we are considering a federal Constitution, the Confederacy is simply not working. "…that something is necessary to be done to rescue us from impending anarchy." He cites various weaknesses as "insufficiency of the present Confederation to the preservation of the Union." These are: unable to pay our debts to foreigners or to our own citizens, we have valuable territories and important imposts that foreigners will not surrender, and we are in no condition to resent or repel them. So representatives from each state assembled to discuss how to change these in order to strengthen us as a nation.

The states had a great degree of independence or even sovereignty under the Articles of Confederation. For a variety of reasons States wanted to hold onto a lot of this power. Most of them strongly guarded this independence. Many delegates held strong positions that the States should have primary powers—that only some powers should be surrendered to a federal government. (See the review of original State Constitutions below.)

In the southern States, primarily South Carolina, North Carolina, and Georgia the reason for holding onto State power was slavery. Their economies depended on the ownership and forced labor of captives of Africans and persons of African ancestry. Northern states, for mostly commercial reasons, did not want a lot of oversight by a strong federal government and also benefitted economically from the chattel enslavement.

In spite of hearing and reading many opinions and arguments these days that the Constitution's words are somehow sacrosanct—that we must study each phrase carefully to discern its meaning—the Constitution is a result of a Grand Compromise. There were many strongly held positions among the delegates.* In order to craft a document that might eventually be ratified by the states, compromises were necessary which resulted in a Constitution that departed significantly from the grand words of Madison and Jefferson. The compromise was that primacy was given to States—not to people or the federal government. The compromise was necessary to get at least nine of the thirteen states to ratify the Constitution. If this was achieved, then it was to become binding on all thirteen.

*In addition to the grand arguments among the Constitutional delegates that are evident when reading the Federalist Papers, I refer the reader to the following works, *Ketcham* and *Labunski*.

Anyway, a lot of powers were left to the States under the Constitution. The framers seemed to justify this by assuming that, contrary to what the federal government may do, the States would act for the benefit of **the people**. We see what this got us. "The people" were apparently property-owning males of northern European ancestry. For example, Rutledge of South Carolina, when discussing a proposal in the Constitutional

Convention to prohibit the import of slaves, said "if the Convention thinks that North Carolina, South Carolina, and Georgia will ever agree to this plan (the prohibition of importing Africans for enslavement after 20 years) unless the right to import slaves is untouched, the expectation is in vain. The **people** of those States will never be such fools as to give up such so important an interest. (see *Ketcham, p. 165*). No doubt Rutledge wasn't including those captive Africans and descendants of Africans when he referred to, "**the people.**"

That the proposed Constitution was a compromise is treated by *Madison* in *Federalist Paper Number 41*. "... but cool and candid people will at once reflect; that the purest of human blessings must have a portion of alloy in them; that the choice must always be made, if not the lesser evil, at least of the GREATER, NOT THE PERFECT, good; and that in every political institution, a power to advance the public happiness involves a discretion which may be misapplied and abused."

Swept under the rug in all this was to never directly say what the writers meant by people. Recall Madison's words, "**the public good, the real welfare of the great body of people, is the supreme object to be pursued.**" Numerous portions of the Federalist Papers asserted, without proof, that State governments were closer to "the people" than would be a federal government, so States should retain a lot of power and the federal government should have limited powers.

This was done by equating "the people" with "States." This made it seem that the convention was adhering to the Preamble and say, "We the people" when what actually was represented was "we the States." In *Federalist Paper Number 39, Madison* writes, "... this assent and ratification is to be given of the people, not as individuals composing one entire nation, but as composing the districts and independent States to which they respectively belong."

But, here, read this. *Hamilton*, writing in *Federalist Paper Number 15*, struggled with whether the Constitution was for the States or for the people. He states, ... "we must resolve to incorporate into our plan those ingredients which may be considered as forming the difference between a league and a government; we must extend the **authority** of the Union to the persons of the citizens—the only proper objects of government."

Hamilton wrote this in the context of arguing that citizens are the only ones that governments can hold accountable to pay taxes. It is not clear what his definition of "citizen" is. If it means all adult residents of the Union, then he is arguing for taxation without representation to that portion of the population that were not allowed to vote, (see below).

According to *Foster*, there was indeed a debate in the Constitutional Convention as to the meaning of "we the people." "It is thus put by the historian Motley: "The Constitution was not drawn up by the States, it was not promulgated in the name of the States, it was not ratified by the States. The States never acceded to it, and possess no power to secede from it. It was 'ordained and established' over the States by a power superior to the States —by the people of the whole land in their aggregate capacity, acting through conventions of delegates expressly chosen for the purpose within each State, independently of the State governments, after the project had been framed." The States did accede to the Federal Constitution. (John Lothrop Motley's letter to the London Times. Rebellion Record, vol. i, p. 210.)" … "The reasons for requiring a ratification by the people of each State instead of the State legislatures were principally the grave doubts as to the power of the State legislatures to delegate to Congress part of the legislative powers vested in them by their respective peoples; but also the intention to deprive those legislatures of all claim to the right of secession, and to give to the Constitution the sanction of a fundamental law ordained by all the people upon whom it operated." *Foster, p. 94*

"Mr. Madison thought it clear that the legislatures were incompetent to the proposed changes. … A law violating a constitution established by the people themselves would be considered by the judges as null and void." *Foster, p. 94.*

As we shall see, however, in spite of the arguments that the Constitution is to be ratified by the people, the body of the Constitution as it written and as it has been largely interpreted over the years is that it gives primacy to states' rights.

This leads to the question, how do we find out what is the public good, the real welfare of the great body of people? The writers would answer, I am sure, by having them vote. So who could vote? Even though I had assumed that I had reasonable knowledge of what the Constitution says, I was surprised that it does not say who can vote. (Amendments 15 and 19 change this to some extent.), What it says is that for the House of Representatives, each state gets to specify which of its citizens are qualified to vote. Article One Section 2, "The House of Representatives shall be composed of members chosen every second year by the people of the several states, and the **electors in each state shall have the qualifications requisite for electors of the most numerous branch of the State legislature**." For the Senate, Section 3 says, "The Senate of the United States shall be composes of two Senators from each State, chosen by the legislature thereof …" The State legislatures in turn were elected by the voters of each State.

This then requires the serious student to go to each of the State Constitutions existing at the time or the earliest available version and find the qualifications for who was eligible to vote for their US representatives and for their State legislators. Here is a summary. The appendix shows more extensive excerpts from each state Constitution dating from around the time of the ratification of the US Constitution. All states had a residency requirement, and so are not shown here.

Excerpts from Early State Constitutions

Connecticut

"All persons who have been, or shall hereafter, previous to the ratification of this Constitution, be admitted freeman, according to the existing laws of this State, shall be electors."

"Every white male citizen of the United States, who shall have gained a settlement in this state, attained the age of twenty-one years, … and have a freehold estate of the yearly value of seven dollars in this state; …." (The rest of the article has to do with service in the militia as another qualification.)

"It being the duty of all men to worship the Supreme Being, the great Creator and Preserver of the Universe, and their right to render that worship, in the mode most consistent with the dictates of their consciences; no person shall by law be compelled to join or support, nor be classed with, or associated to, any congregation, church or religious association. But every person now belonging to such congregation, church, or religious association, shall remain a member thereof, until he shall have separated himself therefrom, in the manner hereinafter provided …"

"Every white male citizen of the United States, who shall have attained the age of twenty-one years, … and shall sustain a good moral character, shall, on his taking such oath as may be prescribed by law, be an elector."

Delaware

"All elections for governor, senators, representatives, sheriffs, and coroners…; and in such elections, every free white male citizens of the age of twenty-two years or upwards, … having within two years next before election paid a county tax, … shall enjoy the right of being an elector, and every free white male citizen of the age of twenty-two years, … shall be entitled to vote without payment of any tax: *Provided* that

[the provision continues saying this does not include military personnel temporarily stationed in the state etc. etc.]"

Georgia: "The representatives shall be chosen out of the residents in each county, … and they shall be of the Protestant religion, and of the age of twenty-one years, and shall be possessed in their own right of two hundred and fifty acres of land, or some property to the amount of two hundred and fifty pounds."

"All male white inhabitants, of the age of twenty-one years, and possessed in his own right of ten pounds value, and liable to pay tax in this State, or being of any mechanic trade, … shall have a right to vote at all elections for representatives, or any other officers, herein agreed to be chosen by the people at large; …."

Maryland

"That the house of delegates shall be chosen in the following manner: All freemen in this state, above twenty-one years of age, having a freehold therein of not less than fifty acres of land, …; or having not less than forty pounds sterling property in the state, and having resided in the county in which he offers to vote, …"

It is interesting what is said and not said in these documents. "Freemen" I am confident, means only men and excludes Africans and African descendants that are held captive and in forced labor. But could a free African or African descendant who possesses the assets specified above vote? Could Indigenous Peoples vote? Could non-Christians vote? This language doesn't say.

Massachusetts Bay

"Every male person being twenty-one years of age, … having a freehold estate …, of the annual income of three pounds, or any estate of the value of sixty pounds, shall have a right to vote in the choice of a representative or representatives for the said town."

"It is the right as well as the duty of all men in society, publicly and at stated seasons, to worship the Supreme Being, the great Creator and Preserver of the universe. And no subject shall be hurt, molested, or restrained, in his person, liberty, or estate, for worshipping God in the manner and season most agreeable to the dictates of his own conscience, or for his religious profession or sentiments, provided he doth not disturb the public peace or obstruct others in their religious worship."

New Hampshire
"Every member of the house of representatives shall be chosen by ballot; and, for two years, at least, next preceding his election shall have been an inhabitant of this state; shall be, at the time of his election, an inhabitant of the town, ward, place, or district he may be chosen to represent and shall cease to represent such town, ward, place, or district immediately on his ceasing to be qualified as aforesaid."

I didn't find the precise wording for who is qualified to vote. As a side note—in 1776, New Hampshire was hoping that relationships with Great Britain would be restored and that they would continue to be a colony. Their (British) governor had departed and so the legislature prepared a Constitution so that the functions of government could go on.

New Jersey
CONSTITUTION OF 1776, That all inhabitants of this Colony, of full age, who are worth fifty pounds proclamation money, clear estate in the same, and …, shall be entitled to vote for Representatives in Council and Assembly; and also for all other public officers, that shall be elected by the people of the county at large.

That there shall be no establishment of any one religious sect in this Province, in preference to another; and that no Protestant inhabitant of this Colony shall be denied the enjoyment of any civil right, merely on account of his religious principles; but that all persons, professing a belief in the faith of any Protestant sect, who shall demean themselves peaceably under the government, as hereby established, shall be capable of being elected into any office of profit or trust, or being a member of either branch of the Legislature, and shall fully and freely enjoy every privilege and immunity, enjoyed by others their fellow subjects.

Constitution of 1844

Every white male citizen of the United States, of the age of twenty-one years, ..., shall be entitled to vote for all officers that now are, or hereafter may be elective by the people; provided, [excludes military stationed in the state who are not residents] no pauper, idiot, insane person, or persons convicted of a crime which now excludes him from being a witness unless pardoned or restored by law to the right of suffrage, shall enjoy the right of an elector.

New York

"Every male citizen of the age of twenty-one years, ...shall be entitled to vote at such .... **But no man of color**, unless he shall have been for three years a citizen of this state, and for one year next preceding any election shall have been seized and possessed of a freehold estate of the value of two hundred and fifty dollars, over and above all debts and incumbrances charged thereon, and shall have been actually rated and paid a tax thereon, shall be entitled to vote at such election. And no person of color shall be subject to direct taxation unless he shall be seized and possessed of such real estate as aforesaid." Bold added. The bar is raised for 'men of color.'

North Carolina

"That all freemen of the age of twenty-one years, ..., and shall have paid public taxes, shall be entitled to vote for members of the house of commons, for the county in which he resides."

"That all persons possessed of a freehold, in any town in this State, having a right of representation, and also all freemen, …, and shall have paid public taxes, shall be entitled to vote for a member to represent such town in the house of commons: provided, …"

"No free Negro, free mulatto, or free person of mixed blood, descended from Negro ancestors to the fourth generation inclusive (though one ancestor of each generation may have been a white person) shall vote for members of the senate or house of commons."

"The thirty-second section of the Constitution shall be amended to read as follows: No person who shall deny the being of God, or the truth of the Christian religion, or the divine authority of the Old or New Testament, or who shall hold religious principles incompatible with the freedom or safety of the State, shall be capable of holding any office or place of trust or profit in the civil department within this State."

Pennsylvania

"In elections by the citizens, every freeman of the age of twenty-one years, …, and within that time paid a state or county tax, …, shall enjoy the rights of an elector: Provided, that the sons of persons qualified as aforesaid, between the ages of twenty-one and twenty-two years, shall be entitled to vote, although they shall not have paid taxes."

Rhode Island and Providence Plantation

"Every male citizen of the United States, of the age of twenty- one years, … and who is really and truly possessed in his own right of real estate in such town or city of the value of one hundred and thirty-four dollars over and above all encumbrances, or which shall rent for seven dollars per annum over and above any rent reserved …

Every male native citizen of the United States, of the age of twenty -one years, who has had his residence and home in this state two years, and in the town or city in which he may offer to vote, …

South Carolina

"Every free white man, of the age of twenty-one years, being a citizen of this State, ... who hath a freehold of fifty acres of land or a town lot, ... or, not having such freehold or town lot, ... hath paid a tax the preceding year of three shillings sterling towards the support to this government, shall have a right to vote."

Virginia

"All freemen in this state, above twenty-one years of age, having a freehold therein of not less than fifty acres of land, and actually residing in the county in which he offers to vote; or having not less than forty pounds sterling property in the state."

"That all men are by nature equally free and independent, and have certain inherent rights, of which, when they enter into a state of society, they cannot, by any compact, deprive or divest their posterity, namely, the enjoyment of life and liberty, with the means of acquiring and possessing property, and pursuing and obtaining happiness and safety ..."

"The right of suffrage in the election of members for both Houses shall remain as exercised at present; ...."

Constitution of 1830

"Every white male citizen of the commonwealth, resident therein, and twenty-one years and upward ...whose tenant for year, at will or at sufferance, is possessed of an estate of freehold in land of the value of twenty-five dollars, and so assessed, to be if any assessment thereof by required by law; and every such citizen, being possessed, as tenant in common joint tenant or preserver, of an interest in an share of land, and having as estate of freehold therein, [blaa blaa blaa.]"

The wording gets so complicated who knows if you were qualified to vote. I guess if you were a white male of twenty-one years and upward, show up at the polls and see what the election judges say.

I did not focus on the religious issue before as a constraint for participating in some state governments—and therefore, the federal government. As we can see, several of the state Constitutions have conditions on either freedom of religion, or more commonly on what religions are acceptable. Some state Constitutions do not have a religious test for voting, but have a religious requirement for being elected to office. So this is really a further restriction on who can represent, "the people."

Another observation. Where state Constitutions were amended or redone in the decades after ratification of the US Constitution, several became more restrictive—more explicit in stating that Africans and persons of African descent did not have the right to vote.

EFFECTS OF VOTER RESTRICTIONS

Let's do a little thought game. First some data.

Here is the makeup of the US population according to data available from the US Census of 1790.

	Number	% of total
Free white males over **16** years of age:	807,094	21
Free white males under 16 years of age:	791,850	20
Free white females	1,541,263	40
All other free persons	59,150	2
Slaves	694,280	18

I assume that since about half the free white males are over 16 years of age, that forty percent of white males are over 21—voting age. I assume that for all the other categories, forty percent are over 21. By this, below is the estimated population over 21 years of age.

	population	Est. No. Over 21	over 21	%
free white males	1,598,944	639,578	41	
free white females	1,541,263	616,505	40	
All other free persons	59,150	23,660	2	
Slaves	694,280	277,712	18	
total population	3,893,637	1,557,455		

Now, suppose that one of the original states called an election. One hundred inhabitants of the state, over the age of 21 (or 22), go to their polling place where the election for their district is being held. Only white men could vote, so from the estimates above, perhaps 40 percent of the population of voting age was white male. All the women and all the Africans and descendants of Africans have to get out of the line. That leaves only 40 people, but maybe add at most, another one or two for "other free persons." To be eligible to vote, one must own some property, real or otherwise or have paid specified taxes. The above data doesn't show property owners but I doubt that more than half of white men met this qualification,* so 20 or so of the 40 must leave and we are down to 20 of the original 100 that came to vote. Religious tests would have disqualified some, so tell a few more to leave.

*One indication of this degree of property ownership is from *Zinn*. "After we make our way through Abbott Smith's disdain for the servants as 'men and women who were dirty and lazy, rough, ignorant, lewd, and often criminal,' who thieved and wandered, had bastard children and corrupted society with loathsome diseases,' we find that 'about one in ten was a sound and solid individual who would if fortunate survive his 'seasoning' work out his time, take up some land, and wax prosperous. ...'" Smith's conclusion is supported by a more recent study of servants in seventeenth century Maryland, where it was found that the first batches of servants became landowners and politically active in the colony, but by the second half of the century more than half the servants, even after ten years of freedom remained landless. *Zinn, pp. 46 & 47.*

Finally, although most state Constitutions are silent on the matter, restricting the voting to white males means that Indigenous People, and other non-European groups would have been barred from voting. (It doesn't even appear that Indigenous People were included in the census.)* So a few more would be disqualified because they were an Indigenous person. By these reasonable assumptions, less than 20 of the 100 people that showed up to vote actually could. Note that the maybe18 percent of the adult population were Africans or descendants of Africans and therefore prohibited from voting.

*The census does not mention Indigenous People, but certainly, they had no voting rights in the 1780s and 1790s. "… the US government imposed unsolicited citizenship on American Indians with the Indian Citizenship Act of 1924, gesturing towards assimilation and dissolving the nations." *Dunbar-Ortiz, p. 169.*

So there you have it. How can they (or we) say that the states represent the people when more than 80 percent of the adult population did not have the right to vote? Were the founders faithful to the grand words of the Declaration of Independence: "That to secure these rights, governments are instituted among men, **deriving their just powers from the consent of the governed**"? **WE THE PEOPLE!**

Alexander Hamilton in Federalist Paper 57 writes, "the aim of every political Constitution is, or ought to be, first to obtain for rulers men who possess most wisdom to discern, and most virtue to pursue, the common good of the society; and in the next place, to take the most effectual precautions for keeping them virtuous whilst they continue to hold their public trust." So now we know who he and the other founders considered having the most wisdom to discern, and most virtue to pursue, the common good of the society—white, property-owning men.

Let's dwell on this a little. Right away we see that women and non-white males (directed at Africans and descendants of Africans) are excluded for just being who they were. Nothing they could do would ever get them qualified to vote. By contrast, among white males, there were various ways they could get qualified—move into the ranks of voters. Buy some land, amass some assets, etc. but still this held out the prospect of some day becoming a qualified voter. (Not considered was how difficult it may have been to move from owning no significant assets to obtaining some, see above.) Indigenous People were ignored where possible when it came to participating in government. Non-Christians—even in some states non-Protestants—could not hold office or in some cases could not even vote.

In Part Three, there is a Note on economic and political conditions in the colonies and the opportunity to vote. These conditions persisted and very much influenced the writing and ratification of the US Constitution.

Even with the best of intentions, it would have been almost impossible to craft a system of government for all people without the voices of the excluded voters.

Some may think it's weird to suggest that captive African and descendants of Africans and indentured servants should have been allowed to vote. NO, what is weird is keeping these people in brutal conditions by "men who possess most wisdom to discern, and most virtue to pursue, the common good of the society." (*Hamilton, Federalist Paper 57*). "All men are created equal," and "we the people of the United States …" are called out as our ideals. How could the Founders write such flowery language and be so blind to the society around them?

The big question, which is impossible to answer, is what would the US Constitution look like if all adults living in the several states were allowed to vote? What would it look like if each adult meeting an age requirement had the right to be elected to the "most numerous branch of the State legislature?" If the other eighty or more percent of the adult population had been allowed to vote—would the Constitution be set up so that "the powers not delegated to the United States by this

Constitution, nor prohibited by it to the States, are reserved to the States respectively or to the people?"

Here is evidence of what the answer would be.

> Cori Bush, Democratic candidate for Congress from Missouri
>
> She is a Black women who has been subject to the lowest of incomes. She is a single mom. She has been without food, been evicted, dealt with no health insurance, etc.
>
> She made the point that having no money is more expensive than having money. So if she can't afford car insurance and then later on has an accident, it is going to cost her more than if she had insurance. If she can't afford fruits and vegetables so instead buys spam, etc. she is going to have poor health, get diabetes, heart disease, etc. which costs way more than buying the fruits and vegetables.

I did not focus on the following passage in my initial review of the Federal Papers. After working through this section I now see it is an important paper in understanding the development of the Constitution. *John Jay, in Federalist Paper 2* writes: "It has often given me pleasure to observe, that independent America was not composed of detached and distant territories, but that one connected, fertile, wide-spreading country was the portion of our western sons of liberty. Providence has in a particular manner blessed it with a variety of soils and productions, and watered it with innumerable streams, for the delight and accommodation of its inhabitants. A succession of navigable waters forms a kind of chain round its borders, as if to bind it together; while the most noble rivers in the world, running at convenient distances, present them with highways for the easy communication of friendly aids, and the mutual transportation and exchange of their various commodities."

"With equal pleasures I have as often taken notice, that Providence has been pleased to give this one connected country to one united people—a people descended from the same ancestors, speaking the same language, professing the same religion, attached to the same principles of government, very similar in their counsels, arms, and efforts, fighting side by side throughout a long and bloody war, have nobly established general liberty and independence."

It is not a great leap to read this as saying that God had provided a most bounteous and beautiful land to a chosen group of White people. This thinking seems to have permeated the development of our government.

As a side-note to this discussion, for State militias that were prevalent at the time, "the militias were military forces drawn from the citizenry— largely the yeoman farmers who owned property and worked their land." *Waldman, p. 6.* This was a further separation of those who had from those who didn't.

THE STRUGGLES WITH DEFINING "WE THE PEOPLE" AND JUSTIFICATION OF STATES' RIGHTS

The Tenth Amendment states that, "the powers not delegated to the United States by the Constitution, nor prohibited by it to the States, are reserved to the states respectively or to the people." But in the process of arguing for its adoption, authors of the Federalist Papers had to make strong assertions without backup information or logic that this was the best way of providing for **the public good, the real welfare of the great body of people.** (Note that this wording does not say that the powers of the federal government are **few** and defined those that remain with the states are **numerous and indefinite**, as *Madison* writes in *Federal Paper Number 45.*)

Whether by design or not, the Federalist writers sometimes blurred the lines as to whether they were referring to "the people" or to the state. In *Federalist Paper Number 58*, (*Hamilton* or *Madison*) on how members of the House and Senate, respectively, are to be chosen.

The discussion is on the number of representatives in the House and Senate. Here the argument is that the House is chosen "by the people" and the Senate "by the States." So in some cases, the authors argue that "States" are the best representative of "the people" but here, one body is elected by "the people" and the other by "the States." If the states are good representatives of the people, why have a different way of electing members of the two bodies—the House by direct vote and the Senate by State legislatures? Remember Madison's argument that **the real welfare of the great body of people, is the supreme object to be pursued.**

Below are several more examples.

In *Federalist Paper Number 41*, *Madison* treats the basis for granting of named powers to the federal government. He identifies the following bases for doing so. "1. Security against foreign danger, 2. Regulation of the intercourse between nations, 3. Maintenance of harmony and proper intercourse among the States, 4. Certain miscellaneous objects of general utility, 5. Restraint of the States from injurious acts, 6. Provisions for given due efficacy to all these powers."

But before naming these, he writes of the trade-offs that must be made in any of the arrangements. "This method of handling the subject cannot impose on the good sense of people of America. It may display the subtlety of the writer; it may open a boundless field for rhetoric and declamation; it may inflame the passions of the unthinking, and may confirm the prejudices of the misthinking; but cool and candid people will at once reflect; that the purest of human blessings must have a portion of alloy in them; that the choice must always be made, if not the lesser evil, at least of the GREATER, NOT THE PERFECT, good; and that in every political institution, a power to advance the public happiness involves a discretion which may be misapplied and abused."

In *Federalist Paper Number 39, Madison* writes, "… this assent and ratification is to be given of the people, not as individuals composing one entire nation, but as composing the districts and independent States to which they respectively belong."

He is referring here to how the Constitution is to be ratified. He refers to "people, not as individuals …" "but as composing … States to which they belong …" So when the Second Amendment says, "the right of the people" he seems to mean people composing of States to which they belong. This concept may explain why in the preamble to the Constitution, it starts with, "we the people" when what they meant was "we the States that have gotten permission from the people."

In *Federalist Papers Number 38 and 44, Madison* continues to struggle with States rights versus individual rights. Here are some excerpts.

"Let them speak for themselves. This one tells us that the proposed Constitution ought to be rejected, because it is not a confederation of the States, but a government over individuals. Another admits that it ought to be a government over individuals to a certain extent, but by no means to the extent proposed. A third does not object to the government over individuals, or to the extent proposed, but to the want of a bill of rights."

In his arguments in favor of federal powers Madison has an extensive discussion on how to define and enumerate the powers going to the federal government and those to the States. Madison argues for a system that does not require a complete enumeration of powers going to each—this would be an impossible task. He argues for not a listing, but a test "…no axiom is more clearly established in law, or in reason, than that wherever the end is required, the means are authorized, **wherever a general power to do a thing is given, every particular power necessary for doing it is included.**"

There is a curious statement in his argument. The framers seemed to justify a more restricted federal government and less restricted State Governments. They justified this by assuming that, contrary to what the federal government may do, the States would act for the benefit of **the**

people. But Madison says here, "The truth is, that this ultimate redress may be more confided in against unconstitutional acts of the federal government than of the State legislatures, for the plain reason, that as every such act of the former [the federal government] will be an invasion of the rights of the latter [State governments], these will be ever ready to mark the innovations, to sound the alarm of the people and to exert their local influence in effecting a change of federal representatives. There being no such intermediate body between the State legislatures and the people interested in watching the conduct of the former, violations of the State Constitutions are more likely to remain unnoticed and unredressed." So is he saying that State Governments are more likely to get away with taking unconstitutional acts than is the federal government? I think that has happened.

He goes on, "Several important considerations have been reached in the course of these papers, which discountenance the supposition that the operation of the federal government will by degrees prove fatal to the State governments. The more I resolve the subject, the more fully I am persuaded that the balance is much more likely to be disturbed by the preponderancy of the last than by the first scale."

So this says the issue of federal versus state powers is not obviously one way or the other, but is a matter of judgement (the more fully **I am** persuaded). This comes from, "the father of the Constitution."

It gets more complicated. Read what Alexander *Hamilton,* says in *Federalist Paper Number 15.* He states "The great and radical vice in the construction of the existing Confederation is in the principle of LEGISLATION for STATES or GOVERNMENTS, in the CORPORATE or COLLECTIVE CAPACITIES and as contradistinguished from the INDIVIDUALS of which they consist. Though this principle does not run through all the powers delegated to the Union, yet it pervades and governs those on which the efficacy of the rest depends … "we must resolve to incorporate into our plan those ingredients which may be considered as forming the difference between a league and a government; we must extend the authority of the Union to the persons of the citizens—the only proper objects of government.

He continues in *Federalist Paper Number 16*. The Paper challenges my reading comprehension, but here is the essence of the Paper.

"… the principle of legislation for sovereign States, supported by military coercion, has never been found effectual. It has rarely been attempted to be employed, but against the weaker members; and in most instances attempts to coerce the refractory and disobedient have been the signals of bloody wars, in which one half of the confederacy has displayed its banners against the other half."

"The result of these observations to an intelligent mind must be clearly this, that if it be possible at any rate to construct a federal government capable of regulating the common concerns and preserving the general tranquility, it must be funded, as to the object committed to its care, upon the reverse of the principle contended for by the opponents of the proposed Constitution. **It must carry its agency to the persons of the citizens**. It must stand in need of no intermediate legislations, but must itself be empowered to employ the arm of the ordinary magistrate to execute its own resolutions. The majesty of the national authority must be manifested through the medium of the courts of justice. The government of the Union, like that of each State, must be able to address itself immediately to the hopes and fears of individuals; and to attract to its support those passions which have the strongest influence upon the human heart. It must, in short, possess all the means, and have a right to resort to all the methods, of executing the powers with which it is entrusted, that are possessed and exercised by the government of the particular States."

What he is arguing is that when it comes to compelling obedience to federal law, the government must go directly to the people rather than going through the states. He is saying that the federal government has no power over states when it comes to federal law. **So when people wish to express their preferences to the federal government, they must go**

through the states. But when the federal government wishes to compel obedience, it should go directly to the people.

This continues in *Federalist Paper Number 21* where *Hamilton* takes a hard line against those that want to severely limit the powers of the Federal government. "The next most palpable defect of the [Confederacy] is the total want of a sanction of law. The United States, as now composed, have no powers to exact obedience, or punish disobedience to their resolutions, either by pecuniary mulets, by a suspension or divestiture of privileges, or by any other Constitutional mode. There is no express delegation of authority to them to use force against delinquent members; and if such a right should be ascribed to the federal head, as resulting from the nature of the social compact between the States, it must be interference and construction, in the face of that part of the second article, by which it is declared, 'that every State shall retain every power, jurisdiction, and right, not expressly delegated to the United States in Congress assembled.'" ...

"Without a guaranty the assistance to be derived from the Union in repelling those domestic dangers which may sometimes threaten the existence of the State Constitutions, must be renounced. Usurpation may rear its crest in each State, and trample upon the liberties of the people, while the national government could legally do nothing more than behold its encroachment with indignation and regret. A successful faction may erect a tyranny on the ruins of order and law, while no succor could constitutionally be afforded by the Union to the friends and supporters of the government."

The fact that Hamilton placed so much emphasis on this issue, confirms that there was strong resistance from state delegates to granting of powers to the Union.

In *Federalist Paper Number 9, Alexander Hamilton* provides a discussion of arguments for strong individual States. He argues that these make representation of the people more likely.

"This form of government is a convention by which several smaller *States* agree to become members of a larger *one*, which they intend to form. It is a kind of assemblage of societies that constitute a new one, capable of increasing, by means of a new associations, till they arrive at such a degree of power as to be able to provide for the security of the united body."

He goes on to state that a republic of this kind, can also prevent a single State from usurping the authority of the larger body.

"The proposed Constitution, so far from implying the abolition of the State governments, makes them constituent parts of the national sovereignty, by allowing them a direct representation in the Senate, and leaves in their possession certain exclusive and very important portions of sovereign power. This fully corresponds, in every rational import of the terms, with the idea of a federal government."

My comment: So this goes at least part way in justifying State sovereignty. It does not say that the powers of the **National government should be few and defined and those of the States numerous and indefinite.**

In *Federalist Paper Number 45, Madison* expresses concerns that a strong National government is in danger of taking powers that kings have in Europe—a great concern of the Constitution writers. But based on Madison's argument above, it is not the form of government that is ultimately important, it is the results—the consequences of having that government.

Look again at Amendment Ten: The powers not delegated to the United States by the Constitution nor prohibited by it to the States, are reserved to the States respectively or to the people.

Even this seems less restrictive than *Federalist Paper Number 45* language. Repeating No. 45: "The powers delegated by the proposed Constitution to the federal government are few and defined. Those which remain with the State governments are numerous and indefinite." The Constitution does not say United States powers are "few."

This wording is not terribly different from Article Two of the Articles of Confederation, which the Constitution was designed to replace.

"Each State retains its sovereignty, freedom, and independence, and every power, jurisdiction, and right, which is not by the Confederation expressly delegated to the United States in Congress assembled."

The main point here is that Madison—if Federalist Paper 45 is internally consistent—made the case for limited Federal powers because he concluded that arrangement would best advance **the public good, the real welfare of the great body of people, is the supreme object to be pursued.** Of course, we must also note that compromise was necessary to come to a decision so that the body can move forward.

When Congress was voting to add the Bill of Rights amendments to the Constitution, Madison had to fend off a more restrictive provision than he had penned in *Federalist Paper 45*. "Tucker, of South Carolina wanted to place the word "expressly" in what would become the Tenth Amendment to confirm that the federal government was one of limited powers. ..." *Labinski, p. 230*

"Madison vigorously objected, arguing that 'it was impossible to confine a government to the exercise of express powers [;] there must necessarily be admitted powers by implication, unless the constitution descended to recount every minutiae.'" *Labinski, p. 230*

The authors of *Federalist Paper Number 52, Hamilton* or *Madison* deal with the method of electing and the qualifications for being elected to the House of Representatives.

"The first view to be taken of this part of the government relates to the qualifications of the electors and the elected." "The definition of the right of suffrage is very justly regarded as a fundamental article of republican government. It was incumbent on the convention, therefore, to define and establish this right in the Constitution." ... "To have reduced the different qualifications in the different States to one uniform rule would probably have been as unsatisfactory to some of the States as it would have been difficult to the convention. The provision made by the convention appears to be the best that lay within their option."

So, Hamilton is saying that, even if the Founders may have wanted to provide for Federal qualifications for voting, the Convention could never have agreed to what these would be.

US Constitution, Article One, Section 2. "The House of Representatives shall be composed of members chosen every second year by the people of the several States, and the electors (that's us) in each State shall have the qualifications requisite for electors of the most numerous branch of the State legislature."

Further evidence that this is a states' rights Constitution, rather than a peoples' Constitution because if a State decided to restrict eligible voters for congressmen, the original Constitution would allow that as long as the same eligibility requirements applies to electing "the most numerous branch of the State legislatures."

The author(s) are saying this is about the best they can do to get a provision that all states would accept. He or they say that this is a safe way of doing this because the State provisions, he asserts, are in the State Constitutions.

In *Federalist Paper Number 57, Hamilton* or *Madison*, try to tamp down the objections to the way Congressmen are to be chosen. "The third charge against the House of Representatives is, that it will be taken from the class of citizens which will have least sympathy with the mass of the people, and be most likely to aim at an ambitious sacrifice of the many to the aggrandizement of the few."

"Of all the objections which have been framed against the federal Constitution, this is perhaps the most extraordinary. Whilst the objection itself is levelled against a pretended oligarchy, the principle of it strikes at the very root of republican government." "The aim of every political Constitution is, or ought to be, **first to obtain for rulers men who possess most wisdom to discern, and most virtue to pursue, the common good of the society**; and in the next place, to take the most effectual precautions for keeping them virtuous whilst they continue to hold their public trust. The elective mode of obtaining rulers is the characteristic policy of republican government. The means relied on in this form of government for preventing their degeneracy are numerous and various. The most effectual one is such a limitation of the term of appointments as will maintain a proper responsibility to the people."

Of all the arguments made in the Federalist Papers, this is the most egregious. Recall in the earlier section how voters and candidates for office were determined by State Constitutions. All of them had severe restrictions on voting and qualifications for public office. The grand presumption was that "to obtain rulers men who possess most wisdom to discern, and most virtue to pursue, the common good of society;" meant to choose from that 20 percent or less of the population that was 1) male, 2) white, 3) property owner, and 4) Christian to take the most common restrictions. **Women, African and African descendants, laborers, indentured servants, Indigenous Peoples, non-Christians, were thereby presumed to not be in possession of "wisdom to discern, and most virtue to pursue the common good of society."** Africans and African descendants were specifically called out because they were property. In *Federalist Paper Number 54*, it seems grudgingly, affirms that they are also people.

Zinn, quoting *Beard* relates, "the rich must, in their own interest, either control the government directly or control the laws by which government operates. Beard applies this general idea to the Constitution, by studying the economic backgrounds and political ideas of the fifty-five men who gathered in Philadelphia in 1787 to draw up the Constitution. He found that a majority of them were lawyers by profession, that most of them were men of wealth, in land, slaves, manufacturing, or shipping, that half of them had money loaned out at interest, and that forty of the fifty-five had government bonds, according to records of the Treasury Department. Thus Beard found that most of the makers of the Constitution had some direct economic interest in establishing a strong federal government: the manufacturers needed protective tariffs, the moneylenders wanted to stop the use of paper currency to pay off debts, the land speculators wanted protection as they invaded Indian lands, slaveowners needed federal security against slave revolts and runaways, bondholders wanted a government able to raise money by nationwide taxation to pay off the above bonds. Four groups Beard noted, were not represented in the Constitutional Convention: slaves, indentured servants, women, and men without property: And so the Constitution did not reflect the interest of those groups." *Zinn* pp. 90-91.

"When economic interest is seen behind the political clauses of the Constitution, then the document becomes not simply the work of wise men trying to establish a decent and orderly society, but the work of certain groups trying to maintain their privileges, while giving just enough rights and liberties to the people to ensure popular support." *Zinn, p. 96 & 97.*

One might think that the issue of voter enfranchisement was settled if the Fourteenth Amendment is taken at face value. Section 1—"all persons born or naturalized in the United States, and subject to the jurisdiction thereof, are citizens of the United States and of the State wherein they reside. No State shall make or enforce any law which shall abridge the privileges or immunities of citizens of the United States; nor shall any State deprive any person of life, liberty, or property, without due process of law; not deny to any person within its jurisdiction the equal protection of the laws."

Continuing with *Federalist Paper Number 57*, a reader of the following paragraphs, without digging into who may be an elector can easily be convinced of a great democracy to be instituted by the Constitution. An adult reading this Paper at the time might justifiably believe that he now has the right to vote or to become a candidate for office.

"Who are to be the electors of the federal representatives? Not the rich, more than the poor, not the learned, more than the ignorant, not the haughty heirs of distinguished names, more that the humble sons of obscurity and unpropitious fortune. The electors are to be the great body of the people of the United States. They are to be the same who exercise the right in every state of electing the corresponding branch of legislature of the State."

"Who are the objects of popular choice? Every citizen whose merit may recommend him to the esteem and confidence of his country. No qualification of wealth, of birth, of religious faith, or of civil profession is permitted to fetter the judgement or disappoint the inclination of the people."

One can imagine that if a proponent of the Constitution were speaking, he would hurriedly and maybe in a mumbling voice say that everyone can vote for a congressman that possesses the right to vote for state representatives. The speaker would hope no one asks about enfranchisement at the State level.

Hamilton in *Federalist Paper 71* writes, "**The representatives of the people, in a popular assembly, seem sometimes to fancy that they are the people themselves,** and betray strong symptoms of impatience and disgust at the least sign of opposition from any other quarter; as if the exercise of its rights, by either the executive or judiciary, were a breach of their privilege and an outrage to their dignity. They often appear disposed to exert an imperious control over the other departments; and as they commonly have the people on their side, they always act with such momentum as to make it very difficult for the other members of the government to maintain the balance of the Constitution."

From: *John Stuart Mill**, "From these accumulated considerations it is evident that the only government which can fully satisfy all the exigencies of the social state is one in which the whole people participate; that any participation, even in the smallest public function, is useful; that the participation should everywhere be as great as the general degree of improvement of the community will allow; and that nothing less can be ultimately desirable than the admission of all to a share in the sovereign power of the state. But since all cannot, in a community exceeding a single small town, participate personally in any but some very minor portions of the public business, it follows that the ideal type of a perfect government must be representative." *Mill, Chapter 3.*

And "The meaning of representative government is, that the whole people, or some numerous portion of them, exercise through deputies periodically elected by themselves, the ultimate controlling power, which, in every Constitution, must reside somewhere." *Mill, Chapter 5.*

*John Stuart Mill was a politician/philosopher in the 1800's.

Federalist Paper Number 62 (*Hamilton* or *Madison*) goes on to discussing the construction of the Senate. "In this spirit it may be remarked, that the equal vote allowed to each State is at once a Constitutional recognition of the portion of sovereignty remaining in the individual States, and an instrument for preserving that residuary sovereignty. So far the quality ought to be no less acceptable to the large than to the small States; since they are not less solicitous to guard, by every possible expedient, against an improper consolidation of the States into one simple republic."

The author presumes, without analysis that "consolidation of the States into one simple republic" is a bad thing. Nor is this a simple either/or. There can be other arrangements of political units to the federal government. Canada has provinces, which I presume, have fewer powers than our States.

As experience has shown over the 230 or so years of living under the US Constitution, persons with economic and political power want to be left alone by government and thus favor a weak federal government. More specifically, they want to be left alone unless there is something they want and can control what the government does to help them. Persons with little power hope for a lot of government to provide protection from the powerful. An aspect of having little power and few resources is that when disasters and tragedies occur you have limited means of dealing with the event and so are hopeful that government can come to your assistance.

The experience of US history is that the federal government has given some power to the powerless—the Civil War, passage of thirteenth, fourteenth and fifteenth Constitutional amendments, women's suffrage, power to labor unions, and civil rights court cases and legislation, all promulgated by the federal government. It is true that some states set precedence, but it was the federal government that extended these to all citizens. States on the other hand, have been the source of some of the most heinous acts of depriving people of basic rights and dignity—the most obvious is enslavement and the Jim Crow era that followed. At the present time, several states are actively working to deprive classes of citizens the right to vote under the guise of preventing voter fraud.

How are States' rights working to protect "the people"? Industrialists moved plants from the North to the South to escape the power of labor unions. So the workers in the North were hurt by losing their jobs. The workers in the South were hurt by having to work with lower wages and not having the other protections that unions had achieved in the North, such as worker safety and healthy working conditions. It is entirely legitimate, in my view, that companies move operations for strictly economic reasons, such as being closer to supplies or closer to markets. Saving money on the backs of workers is not legitimate. Federal laws requiring that workers have the same rights in all States would have alleviated this problem

Of course, this federal/state characteristic is not all one-sided. Many federal programs have been very discriminatory toward Blacks and others—restrictions on where Black people can purchase housing and get federally guaranteed mortgages, penalties for illegal drugs, etc. I will discuss more fully later, in Part Three, but as a grand general case, strong state's rights works for citizens with political and economic power—not so much for those without these. The powerful are served by States rights, the less powerful are served by a strong federal government.

So with the objective to "obtain for rulers men who possess most wisdom to discern, and most virtue to pursue, the common good of the society," why hasn't this means of maintaining "a proper responsibility to the people," often not worked? With all the knaves, incompetents, oppressors, thieves, egomaniacs, etc. being elected to—and more importantly—re-elected to office time after time, something has not worked right.

The means of maintaining "a proper responsibility to the people," has not worked because only a select portion of the population is franchised. A broader electorate who believed their vote would make a difference would be more likely to weed out the people this Paper said would be weeded out.

Part Two

A Search for Answers in the Federalist Papers

THREE QUESTIONS PLUS ONE

1. Where in these papers, is there justification for a limited National government and more unlimited State governments?
2. Does "no laws abridging free speech" (from Article One of the Constitution) mean we are condemned to having money decide elections?
3. Where do these papers say that we cannot limit who owns and uses firearms?

I am adding a fourth issue here, that of gerrymandering.

One reason why a search through the Federalist Papers does not provide a lot of guidance on these questions is because the first ten amendments—the Bill of Rights—did not exist when the Federalist Papers were written. This is glossed over by proponents who urge that these papers are THE interpretation of the Constitution.

Where in these papers, is there justification for a limited National government and more unlimited State governments?

There are many references in the Federalist Papers about the benefits of a limited federal government. Much rarer is a reasoned argument as to why this is true. Below is a search through the Papers for reasons why we should have a limited Federal Government. But first, let's see what the Constitution says.

Look again at Amendment Ten:

"The powers not delegated to the United States by the Constitution nor prohibited by it to the States, are reserved to the States respectively or to the people."

For all the weight that proponents of limited or small government put on this provision, the amendment is shockingly weak. Compare this language to of Amendment One; "Congress shall make no law …"

One way of reading these words is that if the states do not agree with a Federal law, they must prohibit the Federal Government from enacting the law.

How is it to be handled when "the United States" oversteps its authority and does something "prohibited by it to the States?" Do the States go after the Federal government? How many of them does it take to act against this usurpation? One? Nine? Thirteen? And what entity of the State? The State legislature? Or are the US Senators to act as an "assembly of States" to overturn the prohibited Federal action? If so, again, how many States must vote to take an action? What if the prohibited Federal action is taken by a branch of Congress? Must Congress recuse itself? I have no clue of the answer to any of these questions. Of course, cases can be taken to court, but if the Founders were so greatly concerned about the Federal Government overstepping its authority as provided in the Constitution its seems they would have provided a more explicit way for States to exercise their power.

What are the powers delegated to the United States? Articles One through Six of the Constitution—primarily establishing the three branches of the Federal government—move seamlessly between procedural rules for each branch and powers that each has. **One might expect that if it was so important to lay out just what the Constitution was empowering the Federal government to do, these would be more distinct and highlighted.**

To test out a case, let's assume that in 1802, Congress enacted a law giving women the right to vote and hold US office. (Date chosen to predate Amendment Nineteen) We already know that Article One, Section 2 says, ..."the electors of each State shall have the qualifications requisite for electors of the most numerous branch of the State legislature," and that women were prohibited from voting in all States.

Section 4 says, "The times, places, and manner of holding elections for Senators and Representatives shall be prescribed in each State by the legislature thereof; but the Congress may at any time by law make or alter such regulations, except as to the places of choosing Senators." Does this mean "manner of holding elections" includes prescribing who can vote?

And Article Four, Section 2 says, "The citizens of each State shall be entitled to all privileges and immunities of citizens in the several States."

What if one State in 1802 enacted a law that gave women the right to vote? Would this then apply to all States? I am sure legal experts have answers.

Going now to the Federalist Papers, I do not find in any well-argued justification for restricting the Federal Government from enacting laws not delegated by the Constitution. I am looking for a showing with some examples or "facts" that "the great happiness of the people" is best served by a restricted federal government and more unrestricted State Governments.

In the Federalist Papers, there are many more arguments for establishing a strong federal government than there are for limiting that government. There may be reasons why this is so, but let the proponents of limited government make their case.

Proponents of a limited Federal Government prefer the more expansive language in *Federalist Paper Number 45*, rather than The Tenth Amendment. "The powers delegated by the proposed Constitution to the federal government are few and defined. Those which remain with the State governments are numerous and indefinite."

Let's look through the Federalist Papers for more arguments.

Alexander Hamilton, in Federalist Paper Number 9, writes, "The proposed constitution, so far from implying the abolition of the State governments, makes them constituent parts of the national sovereignty, by allowing them a direct representation in the Senate, and leaves in their possession certain exclusive and very important portions of sovereign power. This fully corresponds, in every rational import of the terms, with the idea of a federal government."

My comment: So this goes at least part way in arguing for State sovereignty. It does not say, yet, that the powers of the **National government should be few and defined and those of the States numerous and indefinite**. We shall see if this construction grows as more Federalist Papers are written.

Hamilton, in *Federalist Paper Number 17*, states, "The regulation of the mere domestic police of a State appears to me to hold out slender allurements to ambition. Commerce, finance, negotiation, and war seem to comprehend all the objects which have charms for minds governed by that passion; and all the powers necessary to those objects ought, the first instance, to be lodged in the national depository. The administration of private justice between the citizens of the same State, the supervision of agriculture, and of other concerns of a similar nature, all those things, in short, which are proper to be provided for by local legislation, can never be desirable cares of a general jurisdiction. It is therefore improbable that there should exist a disposition in the federal councils to usurp the powers with which they are connected; because the attempt to exercise those powers would be as troublesome as it would be nugatory; and the possession of them, for that reason, would contribute nothing to the dignity, to the importance, or to the splendor of the national government."

Comment: This argument is one of mere efficiency of administration. It is not an argument for state sovereignty.

Federalist Paper Number 39, by *Madison* states, "But if the government be national with regard to the *operation* of its powers, it changes its aspect again when we contemplate it in relation to the *extent* of its powers. The idea of a national government involves in it, not only an authority over the individual citizens, but an indefinite supremacy over all person and things, so far as they are object of lawful government. Among a people consolidated into one nation, this supremacy is completely vested in the national legislature. Among communities united for particular purposes, it is vested partly in the general and partly in the municipal legislatures. In the former case, all local authorities are subordinate to the supreme and may by controlled, directed, or abolished by it at pleasure. In the latter, the local or municipal authorities form distinct and independent portions of the supremacy, no more subject, within their respective spheres, to the general authority than the general authority is subject to them within their own sphere. **In this relation, then, the proposed government cannot be deemed a national one; since its jurisdiction extends to certain enumerated objects only, and leaves to the several States a residuary and inviolable sovereignty over all other objects.**"

Again, this explains why the proposed system is not a national system, but nothing here shows why this arrangement will best provide for "the great happiness of the people." And he does not explain why he believes that, "a national government"… having …"an authority over the individual citizens, but an indefinite supremacy over all person and things, so far as they are object of lawful government," is to be preferred over state jurisdiction. I can't help but think here of the treatment of persons of African descent, especially in the southern states, both during the captive period and continuing on into the 1960's and beyond.

Next, in *Federalist Paper Number 41, Madison* treats the basis for granting of named powers to the federal government. He identifies the following bases for doing so. "1. Security against foreign danger, 2. Regulation of the intercourse between nations, 3. Maintenance of harmony and proper intercourse among the States, 4. Certain miscellaneous objects of general utility, 5. Restraint of the States from injurious acts, 6. Provisions for given due efficacy to all these powers."

But before naming these, he writes of the trade-offs that must be made in any of the arrangements. "This method of handling the subject cannot impose on the good sense of people of America. It may display the subtlety of the writer; it may open a boundless field for rhetoric and declamation; it may inflame the passions of the unthinking, and may confirm the prejudices of the misthinking; but cool and candid people will at once reflect; that the purest of human blessings must have a portion of alloy in them; that the choice must always be made, if not the lesser evil, at least of the GREATER, NOT THE PERFECT, good; and that in every political institution, a power to advance the public happiness involves a discretion which may be misapplied and abused." As stated in Part One, the principal author of the Constitution says these arguments are not the best arrangement, but the best that can be done at the time.

In *Federalist Paper Number 44, Madison* continues the arguments in favor of federal powers. There is an extensive discussion on how to define and enumerate the powers going to the federal government and those to the States. Madison argues for a system that does not require a complete enumeration of powers going to each—this would be an impossible task. He argues for not a listing, but a test "...no axiom is more clearly established in law, or in reason, than that wherever the end is required, the means are authorized, wherever a general power to do a thing is given, every particular power necessary for doing it is included."

Here, Madison argues for pragmatism, rather than orthodoxy. When an end is required, the means are authorized to accomplish the end. This is in opposition to those that look on the words and phrases of the Constitution as fixed in stone and must be adhered to regardless of whether they are accomplishing a desired end.

There is a curious Statement in his argument. The framers sought to justify a more restricted federal government and less restricted State Governments. They justified this by assuming that, contrary to what the federal government may do, the States would act for the benefit of **the people**. But Madison says here, "The truth is, that this ultimate redress may be more confided in against unconstitutional acts of the federal government than of the State legislatures, for the plain reason, that as every such act of the former [the federal government] will be an invasion of the rights of the latter [State governments], these will be ever ready to mark the innovations, to sound the alarm of the people and to exert their local influence in effecting a change of federal representatives. There being no such intermediate body between the State legislatures and the people interested in watching the conduct of the former, violations of the State constitutions are more likely to remain unnoticed and unredressed." So is he saying that State Governments are more likely to get away with taking unconstitutional acts than is the federal government? I think that has happened.

Now we come to *Federalist Paper Number 45*, by *Madison*. Citations to this Paper were a primary reason I have taken on the task of reviewing the entire set of the Federalist Papers.

George Will, a political columnist for the Washington Post cited the following from *Federalist Paper Number 45*. "The powers delegated by the proposed constitution to the federal government are few and defined. Those which remain with the State governments are numerous and indefinite." He writes as if this settles the matter.

However, these sentences follows from a long discourse from *Federalist Paper Number 45*, part of which is the following.

"…We have heard of the impious doctrine of the Old World, that the people were made for kings, not kings for the people. Is the same doctrine not to be revived in the New in a different shape—that the solid happiness of the people is to be sacrificed to the laws of political institutions of a different form? It is too early for politicians to presume on our forgetting that **the public good, the real welfare of the great body of people, is the supreme object to be pursued, and that no form of government whatever has any other value than as it may be fitted for the attainment of this object.** Were the plan of the convention adverse to the public happiness, my voice would be, Reject the plan. Were the Union itself inconsistent with the public happiness, it would be Abolish the Union. **In like manner, as far as the sovereignty of the States cannot be reconciled to the happiness of the people, the voice of every good citizen must be, Let the former be sacrificed to the latter.** How far the sacrifice is necessary has been shown. How far the unsacrificed residue will be endangered, is the question before us." (bold added)

Does this sound like Madison is a "States-righter" no matter what?

What I see in Madison's Statement is, first, the welfare of the people, second, what form of government best advances peoples' welfare. Over the years, those in power have argued that States' rights take precedence no matter what because that's in the body of the Constitution.

As I argued in Part One, what should have been done and still should be is to look first to the Preamble when making decisions by the courts, Congress, and the Executive Branch. First consider the vision or goals, then ask and decide how best to accomplish the vision. Remember in *Paper 44*, he argues for not a listing of powers assigned to each level of government, but a test "…no axiom is more clearly established in law, or in reason, than that wherever the end is required, the means are authorized, wherever a general power to do a thing is given, every particular power necessary for doing it is included." So I think from this that Madison would say, whenever the rights of **the great body of people,** are the issue, "wherever the end is required, the means are authorized."

He goes on, "Several important considerations have been reached in the course of these papers, which discountenance the supposition that the operation of the federal government will by degrees prove fatal to the State governments. The more I resolve the subject, the more fully I am persuaded that the balance is much more likely to be disturbed by the preponderancy of the last than by the first scale."

Finally, in *Federalist Paper Number 46, Madison* writes, "Notwithstanding the different modes in which they [the State governments and federal government] are appointed, we must consider both of them as substantially dependent on the **great body of the citizens** of the United States. I assume this position here as it respects the first, reserving the proofs for another place. The federal and State governments are in fact but different agents and trustees of the people, constituted with different powers, and designed for different purposes. The adversaries of the Constitution seem to have lost sight of the people altogether in their reasonings on this subject; and to have viewed these different establishments, not only as mutual rivals and enemies, but as uncontrolled by any common superior in their efforts to usurp the authorities of each other. Truth, no less than decency, requires that the event in every case should be supposed to depend on the sentiments and sanction of their common constituents. "

"Many considerations besides those suggested on a former occasion, seem to place it beyond doubt that the first and most natural attachment of the people will be to the government of their respective States." … "If therefore, as has been elsewhere remarked, the people should in future become more partial to the federal than to the State governments, the change can only result from such manifest and irresistible proofs of a better administration, as will overcome all their antecedent propensities. And in that case, the people ought not surely to be precluded from giving most of their confidence where they may discover it to be most due; but even in the case the State governments could have little to apprehend, because it is only within a certain sphere that the federal power can, in the nature of things, be advantageously administered."

On my. Here Madison says that if the people begin to prefer the federal government over the States, it will be because the federal government does a better job of administration. So if the proponents of deference to State governments wish for the people to prefer States, they should work to make the State governments do a better job of serving the people, rather than disparaging the federal government.

"So far as the disposition of each [State governments and the federal government] towards the other may be influenced by these causes, the State governments must clearly have the advantage. But in a distinct and very important point of view, the advantage will lie on the same side. The prepossessions, which the member themselves will carry into the federal government, will generally be favourable to the States; whilst it will rarely happen that the members of the State governments will carry into the public councils a bias to favour of the general government. A local spirit will infallibly prevail much more in the members of Congress that a national spirit will prevail in the legislatures of the particular States. Everyone knows that a great proportion of the errors committed by the State legislatures proceeds from the disposition of the members to sacrifice the comprehensive and permanent interest of the State, to the particular and separate views of the counties or districts in which they reside. And if they do not sufficiently enlarge their policy to embrace the collective welfare of the particular State, how can it be imagined that they will make the aggregate prosperity of the Union, and the dignity and respectability of its government, the objects of their affections and consultations?"

I don't know where this argument gets us. Is he saying that a federal government won't work because those persons the States send to represent them at the federal level will be more concerned with State issues? Note: my graduate thesis advisor never let me get away with statements like, "everyone knows."

Justifications for more unlimited State governments are better presented in another source—The Anti-Federalist Papers. The writers in these Papers had many reservations about adopting the Constitution and preferred staying with the Articles of Confederation. They make at least a reasoned argument for mostly relying on localized government. "To the anti-federalists, this meant retaining as much as possible the vitality of local government where rulers and ruled could see, know, and understand each other. Thus they cherished the Revolutionary emphasis on state and local councils and committees, and the Articles of Confederation where the central government rested on the states." *Ketcham, p. 17*. Comment: This line of thinking has some surface logic. It would be more valid if the "rulers" got to see, know, and understand all of the "ruled," –women, those at the bottom of the economic order, African and descendant of African captives, indentured servants, renters, Indigenous People, etc.

As mentioned above, there are many more arguments in the Federalist Papers for a strong federal government than there are for a limited federal government. For those interested, below are listed those Papers advocating a strong federal government.

John Jay, Federalist Paper Number 3
John Jay, Federalist Pape Number 4
John Jay, Federalist Paper Number 5
Alexander Hamilton, Federalist Paper Number 6
Alexander Hamilton, Federalist Paper Number 7
Alexander Hamilton, Federalist Paper Number 8
Alexander Hamilton, Federalist Paper Number 9

James Madison, Federalist Paper *Number* 10: The main thrust of the Paper is to show that a republican form of government is the most likely to succeed while providing a system for the people to be heard.

Alexander Hamilton, Federalist Paper Number 11

Alexander Hamilton, Federalist Paper Number 12

James Madison, Federalist Paper Number 13

James Madison, Federalist Paper Number 14

Alexander Hamilton, Federalist Paper Number 15

Alexander Hamilton, Federalist Paper Number 16

Alexander Hamilton, Federalist Paper Number 15, 16, and 17 argue that the federal government must have direct control over individuals to accomplish certain objectives, primarily that of collecting taxes.

Alexander Hamilton and *James Madison, Federalist Paper Number* 20: The authors argue that a strong Union is necessary to discourage and prevent foreign invasion and intervention.

Alexander Hamilton, Federalist Paper Number 21

Alexander Hamilton, Federalist Paper Number 22

Alexander Hamilton, Federalist Paper Number 23:

Alexander Hamilton, Federalist Paper Number 30

Alexander Hamilton, Federalist Paper Number 31

Alexander Hamilton, Federalist Paper Number 32

Alexander Hamilton, Federalist Paper Number 33: Papers *Number* 30, 31, 32, 33, and 36 argue the need to levy taxes directly on the people rather than having the states enforce federal tax laws.

Alexander Hamilton, Federalist Paper Number 34: More on the need for federal authority in taxing. Here, however, he argues for a CONCURRENT JURISDICTION in the article of taxation.

Alexander Hamilton, Federalist Paper Number 36

James Madison, Federalist Paper Number 41

James Madison, Federalist Paper Number 42

James Madison, Federalist Paper Number 43

James Madison, Federalist Paper Number 44

Alexander Hamilton, Federalist Paper Number 59

John Jay, Federalist Paper Number 64. This is in regard to making treaties by the President with the advice and consent of the Senate. I debated whether to include that Paper here as it was uncontroversial that a central government is the proper authority for making treaties. *Alexander Hamilton, Federalist Paper Number 75* makes the same argument.

Does "no laws abridging free speech" (from the First Amendment to the Constitution) mean we are condemned to having money decide elections?

This one is easy to answer, NO! Nowhere in the Federalist Papers is there an argument that "money is speech" as the current argument is made. In fact, the Federalist Papers are virtually silent on any of the rights named in this Amendment.

Where do these papers say that we cannot limit who owns and uses firearms?

For all the attention in modern times given to the Second Amendment, the Federalist Papers say very little. This issue, of course, has been through many court cases, and much political and emotional effort put into it, so what I say here will be immediately challenged.

The first reference to firearms in the Federalist Papers is *Number 29* by *Hamilton*, and this only in passing.

The article refers to the POSSE COMITATUS. This word has gotten to mean groups that go around taking matters into their own hands and generally rebelling against the Federal Government. I think when most people hear this they think of something like vigilantes. But here is what my Random House dictionary says. "*posse comitatus*: 1. the body of men that a peace officer of a county is empowered to call to assist him in preserving the peace, making arrests, and serving writs, 2. A body of men so called to serve."

When I first read the words, I thought maybe Hamilton was justifying our current lunacy of allowing most everyone to have guns. But with the definition of *posse comitatus*, it is obvious that those serving would have been called into service by an arm of the government. This then supports the concept that the Second Amendment should be taken in its entirety—not selecting out a phrase that supports a position. "A well regulated militia being necessary to the security of a free State, the right of the people to keep and bear arms shall not be infringed."

The next Federalist Paper that helps me understand what the framers intended is *Number 41*, by *Madison*. Although the Paper is not specifically about firearms, it strengthens my interpretation. Here, Madison is challenging the logic of including only a part of a proposal as a reason for being against the whole thing. His writing takes some careful reading, but is worth the effort.

"But what colour can the objection have when a specification of the objects alluded to by these general terms immediately follows, and is not even separated by a longer pause than a semicolon? If the different parts of the same instrument ought to be so expounded, as to give meaning to every part which will bear it, shall one part of the same sentence be excluded altogether from a share in the meaning; and shall the more doubtful and indefinite terms be retained in their full extent, and the clear and precise expressions be denied any signification whatsoever? For what purpose could the enumeration of particular power be inserted, if these and all other were meant to be included in the preceding general power? Nothing is more natural nor common than first to use a general phrase, and then to explain and qualify it by a recital of particulars. But the idea of enumeration of particulars which neither explain nor qualify the general meaning, and can have no other effect than to confound and mislead, is an absurdity, which, as we are reduced to the dilemma of charging either on the authors of the objection or on the authors of the

Constitution, we must take the liberty of supposing, had not its origin with the latter."

I take Madison's argument that the general statement sets the meaning, what follows explains the general. "If the different parts of the same instrument ought to be so expounded, as to give meaning to every part which will bear it, shall one part of the same sentence be excluded altogether from a share in the meaning; and shall the more doubtful and indefinite terms be retained in their full extent, and the clear and precise expressions be denied any signification whatsoever?"

I interpret this in the case of the Second Amendment that the whole amendment is what is meant—taking a part of it as having meaning all alone is not what was intended. "… the right of the people to keep and bear arms shall not be infringed" has been posted far and wide for decades. Madison's argument says you cannot take this phrase by itself.

In *Federalist Paper Number 39, Madison* writes, "… this assent and ratification is to be given of the people, not as individuals composing one entire nation, but as composing the districts and independent States to which they respectively belong."

He is referring here to how the Constitution is to be ratified—not to the Second Amendment. However, he seems to refer to "people, not as individuals …" "but as composing … States to which they belong …" So when the Second Amendment says, "the right of the people" I think he means people composing of States to which they belong. This makes the whole amendment consistent—it authorizes State Militias and the people **on behalf of the State** to bear arms."

Finally, in *Federalist Paper Number 46, Madison* concludes by arguing that if the people of Europe had arms in the hands of local jurisdictions, the "throne of every tyranny in Europe would be speedily overturned in spite of the legions which surround it." Note: "in the hands of local jurisdictions," not "in the hands of people acting individually."

Therefore, those arguing against any controls over individuals possessing firearms have a very weak basis in the Constitution or the Federalist Papers.

The current continuing campaign of the NRA for unlimited possession of firearms is of fairly recent origin. This will be covered in Part Three.

The conclusion from answers to Questions 2 and 3 means that proponents of having no limits on campaign spending and possession of firearms **stand the Constitution on its head. Rather than the Constitution being to promote "the great happiness of the people," the interpretations by these proponents requires that the people be harmed by it**. We are told any and all of us must live in constant danger—our children at school, going to a movie, to church, etc. etc. because the Constitution says any person with an evil intent is allowed to have guns.

Likewise, we are told that we cannot really vote for candidates who make the best case that he or she would promote policies and laws in line with our preferences, rather, candidates can be nominated and elected on the basis of which ones have the most to spend.

I conclude the discussion of Questions 2 and 3 by introducing *Federalist Paper Number 84* by *Alexander Hamilton*. Hamilton argues against including a bill of rights in the Constitution. His wording is a premonition of the twisted arguments we get into today—free speech, paying for elections, right for everyone to carry a gun around, etc.

"I further and affirm that bills of rights, in the sense and to the extent in which they are contended for, are not only unnecessary in the proposed Constitution, but would even be dangerous. They would contain various exceptions to powers not granted; and on this very account, would afford a colourable pretext to claim more than were granted." See esp. the Second Amendment. "For why declare that things shall not be done which there is not power to do? Why, for instance, should it be said that the liberty of the press shall not be restrained when no power is given by which restrictions may be imposed? I will not contend that such a provision would confer a regulating power; but it is evident that it would furnish, to men disposed to usurp, a plausible pretence for claiming that power. They might urge with a semblance of reason that the Constitution ought not to be charged with the absurdity of providing against the abuse of an authority which was not given, and that the provision against restraining the liberty of the press afforded a clear implication that a power to prescribe proper regulations concerning it was intended to be vested in the national government. This may serve as a specimen of the number handles which would be given to the doctrine of constructive powers by the indulgence of an injudicious zeal for bills of rights."

Hamilton's arguments against having a bill of rights, if he had won, may have saved as from the follies visited on us that we are forced to let money (corporations are people) buy elections and two, we are prevented from any reasonable actions to control who is allowed to carry and use firearms.

Gerrymandering

Next, we get to the issue of gerrymandering. The term had not even been invented at the time of adoption of the Constitution.

"The word gerrymander (originally written Gerry-mander) was used for the first time in the *Boston Gazette* on 26 March 1812. The word was created in reaction to a redrawing of Massachusetts state senate election districts under Governor Elbridge Gerry. In 1812, Governor Gerry signed a bill that redistricted Massachusetts to benefit his Democratic-Republican Party. In the process of setting electoral districts, **gerrymandering** is a practice intended to establish a political advantage for a particular party or group by manipulating district boundaries. The resulting district is known as **gerrymander** ... however, that word can also refer to the process. The term *gerrymandering* has negative connotations.

Two principal tactics are used in gerrymandering: "cracking" (i.e. diluting the voting power of the opposing party's supporters across many districts) and "packing" (concentrating the opposing party's voting power in one district to reduce their voting power in other districts)."

"In addition to its use achieving desired electoral results for a particular party, gerrymandering may be used to help or hinder a particular demographic, such as a political, ethnic, racial, linguistic, religious, or class group, such as in U.S. federal voting district boundaries that produce a majority of constituents representative of African-American or other racial minorities, known as "majority-minority districts". Gerrymandering can also be used to protect incumbents." *Wikipedia, August 2017*

Essentially, gerrymandering reverses the democratic process. In the democratic process, voters choose candidates and elect persons to office. In gerrymandering, **the candidates choose their voters**, thus usurping the right of voters to vote for their preferences. In today's gerrymandering, Congressional districts are carved up by politicians currently holding office according to expected voting patterns so that a certain candidate or party has a high chance of winning. This has gotten much worse in recent elections where computer searches can identify voting patterns down to extremely small political units. So the politicians can draw Congressional districts very precisely to give a higher chance of winning the next election to the preferred candidate or party. Gerrymandering is shamelessly carried on by both political parties. It makes a sham of democracy.

Gerrymandering is made possible by political parties. The Founders were wary of political factions or what has developed—political parties. Madison knew this was a danger, but hoped to control it by the checks and balances incorporated into the Constitution. It hasn't worked. Here are parts of *Federalist Paper Number 10* that identifies the issue and expresses hope for its control. This deals with the dangerous vice of political factions and how a national government has a better chance of dealing with factions.

"By a faction, I understand a number of citizens, whether amounting to a majority or minority of the whole, who are united and actuated by some common impulse of passion, or of interest, adverse to the rights of other citizens, or to the permanent and aggregate interests of the community." [Our political parties are factions under this overall heading, although there are many other factions in our political life.] He admits that every interest group will be fighting for its welfare rather than the national welfare. The valuable improvements made by the American Constitutions on the popular models, both ancient and modern, cannot certainly be too much admired; but it would be an unwarrantable partiality, to contend that they have as effectually obviated the danger on this side, as was wished and expected. Complaints are everywhere heard from our most considerate and virtuous citizens, equally the friends of public and private faith, and of public and personal liberty, that our governments are too unstable, that the public good is disregarded in the conflicts of rival parties, and that measures are too often decided, not according to the rules of justice and the rights of the minor party, but by the superior force of an interested and overbearing majority. However anxiously we may wish that these complaints had no foundation, the evidence of known facts will not permit us to deny that they are in some degree true. It will be found, indeed, on a candid review of our situation, that some of the distresses under which we labour have been erroneously charged on the operation of our governments, but it will be found, at the same time, that other causes will not alone account for many of our heaviest misfortunes …" Factions are a part of the human condition as many differing talents and interests drive citizens to want different things.

"The instability, injustice, and confusion introduced into the public councils, have, in truth, been the mortal diseases under which popular governments have everywhere perished, as they continue to be the favorite and fruitful topics from which the adversaries to liberty derive their specious declamation."

"It is vain to say that enlightened Statesmen will be able to adjust these clashing interests, and render them all subservient to the public good. Enlightened Statesmen will not always be at the helm."

"The inference to which we are brought is, that the *causes* of faction cannot be removed, and that relief is only to be sought in the means of controlling its *effects*." Madison goes on to discuss how to create a government that alleviates the power of factions. "To secure the public good and private rights against the danger of such a faction, and at the same time to preserve the spirit of and the form of popular government, is then the great object to which our inquiries are directed."

Comment: A proposed way of dealing with factions is that all citizens make their preferences known. This would be done by a true democracy, by this he means a society consisting of a small number of citizens, who assemble and administer the government in person. This supposedly reduces the impact of factions or interest groups. But he argues that in such a pure democracy, a common passion or interest will, in almost every case, be felt by the majority ... and there is nothing to check the inducements to sacrifice the weaker party or an obnoxious individual...

His remedy is a republican (representative) form of government, rather than a democracy (which constitutionally is what we have). "A republic, by which I mean a government in which the scheme of representation takes place, opens a different prospect, and promises the cure for which we are seeking." "The two great points of differences between a democracy and a republic are: first, the delegation of the government, in the latter, to a small number of citizens elected by the rest; secondly, the greater number of citizens, and greater sphere of country, over which the latter may be extended."

Next, he goes to how well representative government might work for various sizes on republics. In the case of small republics, there must be a certain number of representatives to guard against the cabals of a few; and that however large the republic, they must be limited to a certain number, in order to guard against the confusion of a multitude.

"In the next place, as each representative will be chosen by a greater number of citizens in the large that in the small republic, it will be more difficult for unworthy candidates to practice with success the vicious art by which elections are too often carried, and the suffrages of the people being more free, will be more likely to centre in men who possess the most attractive merit and the most diffusive and established character." [I am copying this just after the 2016 presidential election!!!]

"The other point of difference is, the greater number of citizens and extent of territory which may be brought within the compass of republican than of democratic government; and it is this circumstance principally which renders factious combinations less to be dreaded in the former than in the latter. **The smaller the society, the fewer probably will be the distinct parties and interests composing it; the fewer the distinct parties and interests, the more frequently will a majority be found of the same party; and the smaller the number of individuals composing a majority, and the smaller the compass within which they are placed, the more easily will they concert and execute their plans of oppression. Extend the sphere, and you take in a greater variety of parties and interests; you make it less probable that a majority of the whole will have a common motive to invade the rights of other citizens; or if such a common motive exists, it will be more difficult for all who feel it to discover their own strength, and to act in unison with each other.** Besides other impediments, it may be remarked that, where there is a consciousness of unjust or dishonourable purposes, communication is always checked by distrust in proportion to the number whose concurrence is necessary."

Almost before the ink was dry from writing the Federalist Papers, the act of gerrymandering was done by Patrick Henry of Virginia in a fierce election battle in 1789 to keep James Madison from being elected to the US House of Representatives. "The term "gerrymandering" was not added to the nation's political vocabulary until 1812, ... In that respect, Patrick Henry was ahead of his time." "Madison would have a very difficult five weeks ahead of him. Patrick Henry had done an extraordinary job of creating a congressional district in the Piedmont area of central Virginia that would be hostile to Madison and his supporters. When the General Assembly approved the districts in November, the fifth one listed was comprised eight counties, including Madison's home county of Orange and Monroe's [who was also running] Spotsylvania." *Labunski, p. 148*

"To choose the counties that would make up the congressional district, Patrick Henry looked to the results of the voting in March when citizens elected delegates to the Virginia ratifying convention. Almost all the candidates had announced in advance whether they favored or opposed the Constitution. Henry assumed that voters would express their view of the proposed plan by voting for the candidate who most closely represented their position." *Labunski, p. 148.*

My comment: This really shows how damaging gerrymandering is. Gerrymandering seeks to create **"The smaller the society, the fewer probably will be the distinct parties and interests composing it; the fewer the distinct parties and interests, the more frequently will a majority be found of the same party; and the smaller the number of individuals composing a majority, and the smaller the compass within which they are placed, the more easily will they concert and execute their plans of oppression."** As mentioned above, gerrymandering has gotten more pernicious with the modern ability to track voting patterns down to very small political units and areas. After reading *Federalist Paper Number 10*, I am convinced that a great requirement to regain—or really create—a government **of** the people **by** the people **for** the people, is to abolish gerrymandering.

There are a number of ways this could be done. One way is to abolish Congressional districts. Candidates would run state-wide. So if a State has eight Congressional seats, the eight candidates with the greatest number of votes would be elected. Each candidate would have to decide where and how to do his/her campaigning to garner a large number of votes. I am convinced this would dramatically change the make-up of Congress.

Part Three

Going Deeper

I pledge allegiance to the flag of the United States of America
and to the republic for which it stands, one nation,
under God, indivisible, with liberty and justice for all.

Equal justice under the law

All are God's children, and all persons here (and in other countries) are our brothers and sisters—our siblings. But is this what most people think when they say "under God?" Does God tell us to consign large groups of Americans to second or third class citizenship? Does God want us to put elementary school low-income African Americans on a conveyer belt to prison? Does God say we should put persons living here under daily fear that they will be deported and torn from families?

With liberty and justice for all. Oh, okay. So Black citizens don't have to worry about *Driving While Black*? Latinos don't have to worry about Joe Arpaio as long as they are obeying the law?? When brought to court, Black citizens can expect to get the same sentence as a white person for the same offense? All kids can receive the resources in education so that each one graduating from high school has a good basic education and job skills?

Much of the way the Federal Government operates today is the result of laws and customs developed over the centuries since the Constitution was ratified. So what follows may or may not reflect how our system of government functions today. We see, however, that the advocates—and more importantly, the interpretations of these writings—still have a tremendous impact on our nation.

THE FEDERALIST SOCIETY

One of the reasons I started this effort was because of writings by members of the <u>Federalist Society</u>. The <u>Federalist Society for Law and Public Policy Studies</u>, most frequently called simply the <u>Federalist Society</u>, is an organization of conservatives and libertarians seeking reform of the current <u>American legal system.</u> This Society, organized in the late twentieth century urges—with considerable success—that it possesses the knowledge to provide the true meaning of the Federalist Papers and has worked to establish the Federalist Papers as *the* interpretation of the US Constitution. The Society seems to insist that the Federalist Papers have some legal standing—that is, if a court issues a ruling that is in conflict with what is found in the Papers, then the court has erred. Keep in mind that these Papers were nothing more than opinion pieces written by mostly two men—proponents of the proposed Constitution.

I have been troubled by several of Federalist Society positions, so decided to do a deep study of the Papers to find if there are other possible interpretations. I focused on just a few issues, but added more as I did my studies. In many instances, I reach quite different interpretations of the Federalist Papers than does the Federalist Society. So let's look into the Federalist Society.

"The Federalist Society has become kind of mythologized," said Nadine Strossen, president of the American Civil Liberties Union, who often speaks at the group's events. "For those who don't really know what they do, the ACLU can be shorthand for the liberal agenda and the

Federalist Society can be shorthand for the conservative legal agenda." *Fletcher, p. A.21*

"'I think the Federalist Society and some other conservative organizations have played a really important role in changing the terms of legal and, ultimately, political debate in the United States,' said Peter J. Rubin, a Georgetown University law professor and founder of the American Constitution Society, which aims to do for liberals and centrists what the Federalist Society has done for conservatives and libertarians." *Fletcher, p. A.21*

The Federalist Society as a body, takes every opportunity to emphasize the States' rights position in the Constitution. Look again at Amendment 10: The powers not delegated to the United States by the constitution nor prohibited by it to the States, are reserved to the States respectively or to the people.

Compare this to *Federalist Paper Number 45* language. "The powers delegated by the proposed constitution to the federal government are few and defined. Those which remain with the State governments are numerous and indefinite." The Constitution does not say United States powers are "few."

But remember my favorite passage recorded in Part One: "…We have heard of the impious doctrine of the Old World, that the people were made for kings, not kings for the people. Is the same doctrine not to be revived in the New [World] in a different shape—**that the solid happiness of the people is to be sacrificed to the laws of political institutions** of a different form? …It is too early for politicians to presume on our forgetting that **the public good, the real welfare of the great body of people, is the supreme object to be pursued, and that no form of government whatever has any other value than as it may be fitted for the attainment of this object.** Were the plan of the convention adverse to the public happiness, my voice would be, Reject the plan. Were the Union itself inconsistent with the public happiness, it would be Abolish the Union. **In like manner, as far as the sovereignty of the States cannot**

be reconciled to the happiness of the people, the voice of every good citizen must be, Let the former be sacrificed to the latter. How far the sacrifice is necessary has been shown. How far the unsacrificed residue will be endangered, is the question before us."

The <u>Federalist Society</u> argues that the Constitution is unchangeable, that its value is good for all time. But based on the above, would Madison today say that some major changes should be made in our governments so that we can pursue that supreme objective—the real welfare of the great body of people? Would he still argue that, "The powers delegated by the proposed constitution to the federal government are (should be) few and defined. Those which remain with the State governments are (should be) numerous and indefinite."

I suspect that the <u>Federalist Society</u> is selectively interpreting the Federalist Papers and using these interpretations to bolster arguments for limited government, protecting actions of ultra-rich people, etc. From my studies, the Federalist Papers when read to get their intended meaning, more reflect the desire to make this new nation a government of the people, by the people, and for the people. The fault lies, not in their objective, but in their restricted conceptions of who "the people" are (or were). Their concept was white, property-owning men.

The <u>Federalist Society</u>, it seems, insists that these papers show that States should have default powers, that is, if the Constitution does not give a power to the national government, then it cannot expand its powers. This is in contrast to what *Madison* wrote in *Federalist Paper Number 41*, where he treats the basis for granting of named powers to the federal government. He writes of the trade-offs that must be made in any of the arrangements. "This method of handling the subject cannot impose on the good sense of people of America. It may display the subtlety of the writer; it may open a boundless field for rhetoric and declamation; it may inflame the passions of the unthinking, and may confirm the prejudices of the misthinking; **but cool and candid people will at once reflect; that the purest of human blessings must have a portion of alloy** in them; that the choice must always be made, if not the lesser evil, at least of the GREATER, NOT THE PERFECT, good; and that in every political institution, a power to advance the public happiness involves a discretion which may be misapplied and abused."

"The Federalist Society began at Yale Law School, Harvard Law School, and the University of Chicago Law School in 1982 as a student organization that challenged what its members perceived as the orthodox American liberal ideology found in most law schools. The Society asserts that it "is founded on the principles that the State exists to preserve freedom, that the separation of governmental powers is central to our Constitution, and that it is emphatically the province and **duty of the judiciary** to say what the law is, not what it should be." *The Federalist Society*

Comment: How does the bolded phrase square with the Supreme Court initiating the case of Citizens United which removes the last vestige of protection from money buying elections? This case threw out some Federal election laws.

"Northwestern University law professor Steven G. Calabresi, chairman and a founder of the group, said he started the organization after determining that he was one of few conservatives during his student days at Yale Law School. Calabresi envisioned the organization as a vehicle for bringing conservative and libertarian legal thinkers to campus to share their ideas and counteract what he saw as a liberal bias. The idea spread to other schools, notably the University of Chicago, and now there are chapters at the vast majority of the nation's 191 law schools." *Fletcher, p. A.21*

"Through the years, the Federalist Society, which has a $5 million budget, has also received substantial financial backing from a network of foundations that has supported a diverse menu of conservative causes, including promoting school vouchers and investigating the personal life of former president Bill Clinton. These include the John M. Olin and Charles G. Koch foundations. Conservative activist Richard Mellon Scaife is also a major benefactor." *Fletcher p. A.21*

"It has played a significant role in moving the national debate to the right on the Second Amendment, campaign finance regulation, State sovereignty, and the Commerce Clause. It plays a central role in networking and mentoring young conservative lawyers." *Hollis-Brusky p. 213.*

The Federalist Society passes on the suitability of all federal Judges that are nominated to be approved by Congress when we have a Republican president. Think of that! The public is largely unaware of this power that the Society has appropriated. So an unelected organization with a very strict definition of the Constitution and strong conservative views gets to choose our federal judges.

Previously, the American Bar Association reviewed candidates for federal judges, especially Supreme Court nominees and issued an opinion to Congress, which was made public. One may argue against the ABA, which is also an unelected body, passing on the suitability of judges. But at least the process was well publicized. With the Federalist Society acting as a filter, the public is largely unaware of it involvement—rather perhaps thinking nominees are chosen for their judicial accomplishments, rather than their conservative political views. It would be much better if all candidates were evaluated by a number of political and professional organizations and all these evaluations widely publicized.

The extent of wishing to keep the public unaware is shown by the following. "After President Bush tapped John G. Roberts Jr. for the Supreme Court, the nominee was widely reported to be a member of the Federalist Society—an assertion that White House officials vigorously disputed."

"When it was later disclosed that Roberts was once listed as serving on the steering committee of the group's Washington chapter, Bush aides continued to insist that Roberts has no recollection of ever being a full-fledged member of the conservative legal group." *Fletcher. p. A.21*

"In one sense, the key role played by one organization of lawyers in the selection of a Supreme Court justice is remarkable. Typically, the president works with White House and Department of Justice staff in identifying and assessing potential judicial nominees. Interest groups and others weigh in and may have considerable influence, but no single group is dominant. In another sense, the role of the Federalist Society is the natural culmination of a decades long evolution of judicial selection by Republican presidents, one that has made ideological credentials more central to the nomination process." *Baum and Devins*

"That evolution began with the Ronald Reagan presidency. The Federalist Society was founded in 1982 in order to advance conservative ideas in the legal academy and ultimately in the legal system as a whole. From 1985 to 1988, Reagan Attorney General Edwin Meese—an early supporter of the society—helped groom and credential young conservative lawyers by giving key positions in the Justice Department to early leaders of the society. Following a similar path, the George H.W. Bush administration gave responsibility for judicial selection in the White House Counsel's office to Lee Liberman Otis, a founder of the society." *Baum and Devins*

"Federalist Society members also received several nominations to appellate judgeships in the Reagan and Bush administrations. Reagan nominated two of the society's original faculty advisers—Robert Bork and Antonin Scalia—to the U.S. Court of Appeals for the District of Columbia Circuit and the Supreme Court. Bush nominated Clarence Thomas to both courts." *Baum and Devins*

"By the time George W. Bush became president in 2001, though, the Federalist Society had grown in size and prominence. The nomination and withdrawal of Supreme Court nominee Harriet Miers in 2005 further illustrated the power of the Federalist Society in the appointment process. The Miers nomination received public support from Leonard Leo, then as now a leader of the society. But others in the society attacked Miers on multiple grounds, including her lack of ties to the Federalist Society. Writing in the *Legal Times*, for example, Todd Zywicki demanded that Miers withdraw and be replaced by a nominee from the "deep farm team of superbly qualified and talented circuit court judges primed for this moment." Those attacks helped lead to Miers' withdrawal from consideration three weeks after Bush announced her nomination. The new nominee was Alito, not only a Federalist Society member but also a favorite of the conservatives who had criticized the Miers nomination. Alito is a regular speaker at the Federalist Society annual convention and delivered a eulogy for Scalia at the 2016 convention." _Baum and Devins_

The case, of course, is not all one-sided. Here are arguments by supporters of The Federalist Society nominees and opposed to the ABA tradition.

Batkins, cited in a newsletter of the Center for Individual Freedom CFIF, writes, "The Society and other organizations has studies which show that the Bar Association has a liberal bias in its recommendations." *Batkins*.

The Society has a periodical called ABA Watch which goes into great lengths to take issue with the ABA on their judicial ratings. Even though the ABA is no longer used by Republican presidents, the Society remains concerned about its influence. *The Federalist Society*

Comment: Just the existence of the periodical of The Federalist Society ABA Watch, shows how politicized is the process of getting judicial nominees. Which is primary, getting judges with the right political affinity or getting those with judicial accomplishments?

Another commentator writes, "While Democratic Court of Appeals nominees who were clerks on the Supreme Court had an average rating of slightly below "well qualified," similar Republican nominees were rated on average as only "qualified/well qualified." Likewise, of nominees who attended Top 10 law schools and served on their law reviews, Democrats had an average rating as "well qualified/qualified," but Republican nominees were only "qualified/well qualified." Overall, Republican nominees had lower ratings than the nominees of either President Carter or President Clinton." *Lott*

"Moreover, the A.B.A. rating system was a poor guide to how judges will do once they are on the bench. According to The Almanac of the Federal Judiciary's lawyer survey, judges who had "good" judicial temperament got lower A.B.A. ratings than judges whom lawyers rated as only 'fair.'" *Lott*

FEDERALIST PAPERS AS SACRED

Proponents for placing great weight on the Federalist Papers as an essential description of what our government should be do a great disservice to persons (like me) who are not professional historians, political scientists, or the like, but are serious about understanding our national heritage. I first became aware of The Federalist Papers in graduate school in the early 1960's. My wife and I wanted to learn more about the world and so one thing we did was to buy a set of books called <u>Great Books of the Western World</u>. There are 54 volumes containing luminaries of the ancient and near past that we knew about, and many we didn't. Book 43 is titled, "American State Papers, The Federalist, and J. S. Mill." Placing the Federalist Papers right after the American State Papers created in my mind that these were in the nature of canon for proper knowledge of US history, similar to writings that are selected for inclusion in the Bible because these represent the "true religion."

With this imprimatur, it is easy for defenders of the Federalist Papers to treat them as some kind of official documents—even sacrosanct, like sacred text. Perhaps, just like when choosing the writings to go into the New Testament of the Bible, some works about Jesus in the years after his execution, were acceptable, and some were not—even hidden away until discovered in recent decades. Likewise, texts in opposition to the Federalist Papers are not at all well-known—not given any status along-side works such as "American State Papers." But we know there was opposition to the Constitution. Where can we go to get these views and evaluate their merits? Are there any writings by those attending the Constitutional Convention that were in opposition to the positions advocated in the Federalist Papers?

I found only in recent years that there is a history of countering views on how our Constitution should be fashioned. For one, in addition to those who wrote in favor of adopting the Constitution, there were others who wrote in opposition—in total or in major areas. As the proponents took on the name of "Federalists," another group—opponents—came to be called "Anti-Federalists. Some of these essays are included in, *Ketcham, pp. 227 to 356 and Labunski,*

Among Anti-federalists were: John DeWitt,* Samuel Adams,* Elbridge Gerry, Massachusetts, Melancton Smith,* "Cato" sometimes identified as New York governor, George Clinton,* "Brutus" probably Robert Yates, John Lansing, New York. Samuel Bryant,* Pennsylvania, Patrick Henry,* along with George Mason are identified the leaders of the Virginia Anti-federalists, also James Monroe,* William Grayson,* and Richard Henry Lee* of Virginia, Thomas Sumter* and Thomas Tudor Tucker* of South Carolina, and Luther Martin of Maryland. *Labunski, p. 20 and Ketcham, pp. 16 - 20*

The authors of the Federalist Papers while taking strenuous issue with opposing views, did not name those holding other views. Maybe it was the practice to be gentlemanly and not name names, but by doing so, it prevents the student of the Papers from analyzing opposing and differing viewpoints and deciding on the merits of other arguments.

A more complete history and understanding of the early years of our nation would include these writings in the "Great Books" collection and elsewhere as well as the Federalist Papers. Both sets were written by participants to the Constitutional Convention, so each should be equally valid for our history. And, as covered below, I conclude that the Anti-federalists had more influence in shaping the Constitution that was ratified, than did the Federalists.

On a more comprehensive scale, a student of these developing times in our nation needs a more complete general history which provides the

---

* *not listed as Convention delegates by Wikipedia*

political and social environment in which our government was formed. In addition to standard history texts used in high schools and colleges, histories from other perspectives are needed. One such texts is, <u>A People's History of the United States</u>. While most history texts record the major events, especially wars, and persons in important positions of politics, commerce, science, etc., this text writes from the perspective of groups of people living without recognition or power. This work provides a vast pool of knowledge of the condition of the unfamous and those having little or no political power. *(see Zinn)* More recently, we have other texts dealing with people living in the United States, but had (have) almost no political power. One valuable book with a very similar title is, <u>An Indigenous Peoples' History of the United States</u>. *Dunbar-Ortiz*

If we are to understand how our Constitution came to be and how it should be interpreted, we should put other viewpoints along-side the Federalist Papers. To get a more complete picture of the needs and wants of society in the 1787 period, we need to go to other sources.

WHO'S IN—WHO'S OUT?

Political and Economic Conditions at the Time of the Revolution

Economic and social classes were well-established in England prior to the time of settlements in North America. These carried forward in colonial North America and were incorporated into governing systems from the beginning on through the development of the US Constitution and beyond.

To understand how these classes influenced the making of the Constitution, it is necessary to learn more about how the various classes and class structures interacted. For example, *Federalist Paper Number 6*, refers to Shays. "If Shays had not been a *desperate debtor,* it is to be doubted whether Massachusetts would have been plunged into a civil war." The

Papers don't explain what this was all about. In *Zinn*, we learn that the subject was Shay's Rebellion. "In the western towns of Massachusetts there was resentment against the legislature in Boston. The new (state) Constitution of 1780 had raised the property qualifications for voting. No one could hold state office without being quite wealthy. Furthermore, the legislature was refusing to issue paper money, as had been done in some other states, like Rhode Island, to make it easier for debt-ridden farmers to pay off their credit." This source goes on to relate increasing tensions between increasingly organized farmers and the General Court. Daniel Shays, a poor farmer in western Massachusetts and a fighter in the Revolutionary War, became an activist when he saw, among other things, a sick woman had her bed taken from her for non-payment of debts. Shays went on to organize 700 farmers and marched to Springfield. The events continued to escalate for months. In the end, in battles between Shays' groups and those supporting the State, the rebellion was put down and several of Shays' men were hanged. *Zinn pp. 91 – 95*.

So besides the nation's founders who were at the top of the economic and social order, what was the makeup of the rest of the population? An extensive discussion is available in *Zinn, chapters. 2 to 5*—excerpts are below.

One group was the poor from England many of whom came to North America as indentured servants. Indentured servants were white men, women, girls, and boys who were purchased to work for those with means. After several years of service to their owner—or master—the practice was to let these people go free. Many remained poor and formed one of several groups that the elite had to devise ways of control.

Bacon's Rebellion in 1676, according to the Royal Commission's report, was led by frontiersmen and joined by slaves and servants. Bacon was reported as ominous, pensive, melancholy. He seduced the Vulgar and most ignorant people. "The servants who joined Bacon's Rebellion were part of a larger underclass of miserably poor whites who came to North American colonies from European cities whose governments were anxious to be rid of them." Many of these were indentured servants who worked for the master for five to seven years to gain his or her freedom. *Zinn, p. 42.*

The practice of indentured servants sounds like a benign system where a young person might start out with nothing. He or she could learn marketable skills while a servant, then go on to economic self-sufficiency. But read some accounts in Zinn. "Beatings and whippings were common. Servant women were raped. One observer testified: 'I have seen an Overseer beat a Servant with a cane about the head till the blood has followed, for a fault that is not worth the speaking of...'" "The master tried to control completely the sexual lives of the servants. It was in his economic interest to keep women servants from marrying or from having sexual relations because having babies would interfere with work. ... Benjamin Franklin gave this advice to his readers, 'Let thy maidservants be faithful, strong, and homely.'"

"Indentured servants were bought and sold like slaves. An announcement in the *Virginia Gazette*, March 28, 1771, read, Just arrived in Leedstown, the ship Justitia, with about one Hundred Healthy Servants, Men, Women, & Boys ... the sale will commence on Tuesday, the 2nd of April."

"After we make our way through Abbott Smith's (author of *Colonists in Bondage*), disdain for the servants, as 'men and women who were dirty and lazy, rough, ignorant, lewd, and often criminal,' who thieved and had bastard children, and corrupted society with loathsome diseases' we find that about one in ten was a sound and solid individual, who if fortunate survived his 'seasoning' work out his time, take up land and wax decently prosperous. Perhaps another ten percent would become artisans. The rest, 80 percent, were "certainly ... shiftless, hopeless, ruined individuals, either died during their servitude, returned to England after it was over, or became 'poor whites.'" *Zinn p. 47.*

"But after a careful study, Abbott Smith concludes that colonial society 'was not democratic and certainly not equalitarian; it was dominated by men who had money enough to make others work for them.' And few of these men were descended from indentured servants, and practically none of them had been in that class." *Zinn, p. 46*. If the reader wishes to pursue this, Zinn provides many more descriptions of the conditions of servants in several of the colonies, north and south.

With the problem of Indian hostility, and the danger of slave revolts, the colonial elite had to consider the class anger of poor whites— servants, tenants, the city poor, the property-less, the taxpayer, the soldier and sailor. As the colonies passed their hundredth year and went into the middle of the 1700's, as the gap between rich and poor widened, as violence and the threat of violence increased, the problem of control became more serious." *Zinn, p. 53*

The captive Africans and descendants of Africans made up very substantial portions of the population, both north and south. Another major group was the many tribes of Indigenous People that were relentlessly being pushed off their traditional lands. Each of these groups and others that were in severe economic conditions engaged in a number of rebellions and insurrections—sometimes in coordination with other oppressed groups.

"Only one fear was greater than the fear of black rebellion in the new American colonies. That was the fear that discontented whites would join black slaves to overthrow the established order. In the early years of slavery, especially, before racism as a way of thinking was firmly ingrained, while white indentured servants were often treated as badly as black slaves, there was a possibility of cooperation." *Zinn, p. 37*

"'… masters initially at least perceived slaves in much the same way they had always perceived servants … shiftless, irresponsible, unfaithful, ungrateful, dishonest …' And 'if freemen with disappointed hopes should make common cause with slaves of desperate hope, the results might be worse that anything Bacon had done.'" *Zinn, p. 37*

"In the Carolinas, … whites were out-numbered by blacks and nearby Indian tribes; in the 1750's, 25,000 whites faced 40,000 slaves, with 60,000 Creek, Cherokee, Choctaw and Chickasaw Indians in the area. Gary Nash writes: 'Indian uprisings that punctuated the colonial period and a succession of slave uprisings and insurrectionary plots that were nipped in the bud kept South Carolinians sickeningly aware that only through the greatest vigilance and through policies designed to keep their enemies divided could they hope to remain in control of the situation." *Zinn p. 54.*

"It seems quite clear that class lines hardened through the colonial period, the distinction between rich and poor became sharper. By 1700 there were fifty rich families in Virginia, with wealth equivalent to 50,000 pounds (a huge sum those days) who lived off the labor of black slaves and white servants, owned the plantations, sat on the governor's council, served as local magistrates." *Zinn, p. 47.*

With such ugly views of poor whites, all Africans and descendants of Africans, and all Indigenous Peoples, the political landscape followed with the colonies severely restricting citizens' rights to named classes of persons. "By the years of the Revolutionary crisis, the 1760's, the wealthy elite that controlled the British colonies on the North American mainland had 150 years of experience, had learned certain things about how to rule. They had certain fears, but had also developed tactics to deal with what they feared." *Zinn p. 53.*

So, at the time of the writing and ratification of the US Constitution, there were generally three groups in American society. I will call them, the Federalists, the Anti-federalists, and the disenfranchised. The first two groups were represented at the Constitutional convention—the third was not. The Constitution as presented for ratification and what was eventually ratified was a compromise—I would say a Grand Compromise—between the two groups that were involved with its creation and approval. The disenfranchised group(s) has been with us and still is. As described by *Zinn*, groups rebelled before and after this time—most notable small farmers and others trying to make a living at the margins of society, captive Africans and descendants of Africans, and white servants. The makeup of the disenfranchised has changed over the decades and centuries, but the group is still with us.

Of these three groups, the first two had writers who recorded their views. The Federalists had the Federalist Papers. The anti-federalists did not have formal essays, but were recorded by Madison and others in the deliberations of the Constitutional Convention. Their views will be summarized below. The oppressed groups did not have writers for them at the time. Records of the struggles and ambitions of these groups had to be dug out of reports by courts, military campaigns, and other sources charged with controlling these groups. *Zinn* is largely a compendium of much research done in following decades.

First this: "To many Americans over the years, the Constitution seemed a work of genius put together by wise, humane men who created a legal framework for democracy and equality. This view is stated a bit extravagantly, by the historian George Bancroft, writing in the early nineteenth century."

"The Constitution established nothing that interferes with equality and individuality. It knows nothing of differences by descent, or opinion, or favored classes or legalized religion, or the political power of property. It leaves the individual alongside the individual. ... As the sea is made up of drops, American society is composed of separate, free, and constantly moving atoms, ever in reciprocal action ... so that the institutions and laws of the country rise out of the masses of individual thought which, like the waters of the ocean, are rolling evermore."

Another view of the Constitution was put forward early in the twentieth century by the historian Charles Beard (arousing anger and indignation, including a denunciatory editorial in the *New York Times*.) He wrote in his book *An Economic Interpretation of the Constitution*: "Inasmuch as the primary object of government, beyond the mere repression of physical violence, is the making of the rules which determine the property relations of members of society, the dominant classes whose rights are thus to be determined must perforce obtain from the government such rules as are consonant with the larger interests necessary to the continuance of their economic processes, or the must themselves control the organs of government."

"In short, Beard said, the rich must, in their own interest, either control the government directly or control the laws by which government operates."

"Beard applied this general idea to the Constitution, by studying the economic backgrounds and political ideas of the fifty-five men who gathered in Philadelphia in 1787 to draw up the Constitution. He found that a majority of them were lawyers by profession, that most of them were men of wealth, in land, slaves, manufacturing, or shipping, that half of them had money loaned out at interest, and the forty of the fifty-five held government bonds, according to records of the Treasury Department."

"Thus Beard found that most of the makers of the Constitution had some direct economic in establishing a strong federal government; the manufacturers needed protection tariffs, the moneylenders want to stop the use of paper money to pay off debts, the land speculators wanted protection as they invaded Indian lands, slaveholders needed federal security against slave revolts and runaways; bondholders wanted a government able to raise money by nationwide taxation, to pay off the bonds."

"Four groups, Beard noted, were not represented in the Constitutional Convention, slaves, indentured servants, women, and men without property. And so the Constitution did not reflect the interests of those groups. [he forgot to mention Indigenous Peoples]"

"He wanted to make it clear the he did not think the Constitution was written merely to benefit the Founding Fathers personally, although one could not ignore the $150,000 fortune of Benjamin Franklin, the connections of Alexander Hamilton to wealthy interests through his father-in-law and brother-in-law, the great slave plantation of James Madison, the enormous land holdings of George Washington. Rather it was to benefit the groups the Founders represented, the 'economic interests they understood and felt in concrete, definite from through their own personal experiences.' "

"By 1787 there was not only a positive need for strong central government to protect the large economic interests, but also immediate fear of rebellion by discontented farmers. The chief event causing this fear was an uprising in the summer of 1786 in western Massachusetts, known as Shay's Rebellion." (*Beard* quoted in *Zinn pp. 90 – 91*)

Let's be clear. Beard is saying that establishing a government should include not only rules for repression of physical violence, and making of "the rules which determine the property relations of members of society," but for establishing various freedoms and protection of the weak against the strong and providing certain minimum conditions of livelihood.

Anti-Federalist Views. One document that assembles a lot of what transpired at the convention is The Anti-Federalist Papers published in 1986. The anti-federalists came from the same privileged classes as the Federalists. Both were part of the Constitutional Convention. The differences were a struggle for more centralized federal government, led by Hamilton and Madison, and leaving the federal government mainly as it was under the Articles of Confederation which provided for States to have the most of the power. Leaders included Patrick Henry, Melancton Smith, and John DeWitt. *Ketcham, pp. 16 - 20*

In *Federalist Paper Number 63* by *Hamilton or Madison*, members of this "same privileged classes" holds out the Senate as a protector of the people against themselves.

"Thus far I have considered the circumstances which point out the necessity of a "well-constructed Senate" as "sometimes necessary as a defence to the people against their own temporary errors and delusions" because "there are particular moments in public affairs when the people stimulated by some irregular passion, or some illicit advantage, or misled by some artful misrepresentations of interested men, may call for measures which they themselves will afterwards be the most ready to lament and condemn." And, "in these critical moments, how salutary will be the interference of some temperate and respectable body of citizens in order to check the misguided career, and to suspend the blow meditated by the people against themselves, until reason, justice, and truth can regain their authority over the public mind?" It is not too much of a leap here to interpret Hamilton as saying that those franchised to vote must protect the gullible—the disenfranchised—from their own desires.

THE JUDICIARY, ESPECIALLY THE SUPREME COURT

While the Constitution is a legal document, it is much more. It is a political document bringing a nation into being. It is rightfully enshrined in the National Archives and other places of honor. It is an attempt at building a nation with the highest ideals of human dignity and progress. So rather than dissecting each word or phrase as to its meaning to reach decisions, court rulings should start with the basis of the overall intent of the document. The part that seems always to be omitted in Supreme Court rulings is the Preamble.

> WE THE PEOPLE OF THE UNITED STATES, IN ORDR TO FORM A MORE PERFECT UNION, ESTABLISH JUSTICE, INSURE DOMESTIC TRANQUILITY, FROVIDE FOR THE COMMON DEFENSE, PROMOTE THE GENERAL WELFARE, AND SECURE THE BLESSINGS OF LIBERTY TO OURSELVES AND OUR POSTERITY, DO ORDAIN AND ESTABLISH THIS CONSTITUTION FOR THE UNITED STATES OF AMERICA.

The rest of the Constitution, one should be permitted to presume, puts forth how the preamble can best be implemented.

There are at least a couple of ways the Constitution can be viewed. One is that it is a contract, the other is that it is a covenant. A contract is negotiated between parties that have different interests, but each has an objective that the other can help achieve. For a contract, say one party has some building space that she wants to rent out. Another party is looking for some space to rent. The building owner wants to get a high rent, the potential renter is seeking to acquire low-cost space. So the two parties—even though each has a different objective—will come to an agreement in the rental fees.

A covenant is different. There are no adversarial objectives, no one seeking a gain at the expense of the other. In a covenant, all parties have a mutual interest in advancing the whole body. The preamble to the Constitution sounds like the founders are establishing a covenant—we the people. This is a covenant between a government and the people to form a more perfect union. There is no adversarial intent in this statement. This is what I would hope we mean when we say, "one nation … indivisible."

If the Constitution is considered as a contract, there is no need to have august judges sitting on a court to decide cases. Instead it would be better to have newly-minted lawyers who were recently immersed in contract law. These people, having just finished a rigorous course of studies, would be well-qualified to interpret the contract—the Constitution. By contrast, if the Constitution is a covenant, we should have a cross-section of citizens who have demonstrated they have a view of the nation consistent with the grand words* of our Founders when deciding our most pressing cases.

*(all men [persons] are created equal…real welfare of the great body of people, is the supreme object to be pursued…establish justice, insure domestic tranquility, provide for the common defense, promote the general welfare, and secure the blessings of liberty to ourselves and our posterity)

If this is a democratic republic, all of us are "the people." At certain designated times, we call forth from among us people to carry out the functions of government that we have covenanted to have done. They are still "us"—there is no "them."

To get some idea of how the Framers intended for the Constitution to be implemented, it is useful to review their writings on the federal judiciary. *Federalist Paper Number 78* by *Alexander Hamilton* begins a discussion of the judiciary department. It primarily is used to justify the provision that the justices are life-time appointments, as long as they practice "good behavior." I thought I could go through this in short order because supposedly it does not deal with the questions I have been seeking answers for. Alas, it does not appear that way. With the benefit of 200 + years of living under the Constitution, it is obvious to most that the Supreme Court, (a part of the Justice Branch) in spite of dressing in black robes and sitting in a solemn fashion to hear arguments, is not a judicial body, but a **legislature of last resort**. Why else would the Senate get into such battles about Supreme Court nominees? Each side wants the one chosen to favor their political views. The justices by and large comply with this expectation. In today's climate, and I suspect for much of our history, one of the uppermost reasons for voting for a presidential candidate is what political views he or she will look for in a Supreme Court nominee.

It should be noted that *Federalist Paper Number 78* deals more broadly—the federal judiciary—which is the entire system, not just the Supreme Court. All federal justices go through the same approval process—and all have political and philosophical views. The following expresses the optimism of the advocates of the proposed Constitution.

"Whoever attentively considers the different departments of power must perceive that, in a government in which they are separated from each other, the judiciary, from the nature of it functions, will always be the least dangerous to the political rights of the Constitution; because it will be least in a capacity to annoy or injure them. The Executive not only dispenses the honours, but holds the sword of the community. The legislature not only commands the purse, but prescribes the rules by which the duties and rights of every citizen are to be regulated. The judiciary, on the contrary, has no influence over either the sword or the purse; no direction either of the strength or of the wealth of the society. And can take no active resolution whatever. It may truly be said to have neither FORCE nor WILL, but merely judgement; and must ultimately depend upon the aid of the executive arm even for the efficacy of its judgements."

"This simple view of the matter suggests several important consequences. It proves incontestably that the judiciary is beyond comparison the weakest of the three departments of power; that it can never attack with success either of the other two; and that all possible care is requisite to enable it to defend itself against their attacks. **It equally proves that though individual oppression may now and then proceed from the courts of justice, the general liberty of the people can never be endangered from that quarter; I mean so long as the judiciary remains *truly distinct* from both the legislature and the Executive."**

So there you have it. For how much of our history has this been true? In some instances, the Supreme Court has done irreparable damage to the people over the centuries. Here are some: the Dred Scott decision where it was declared that no person of African descent had any right to citizenship; Plessy vs. Ferguson where it upheld state racial segregation laws for public facilities under the doctrine of "separate but equal"; rulings against the rights of Indigenous Peoples, in our times, the Court held in Citizens United that freedom of speech prohibited the government from restricting independent political expenditures by nonprofit corporations, for-profit corporations, labor unions and other associations. This last case was initiated by the Supreme Court—not the usual manner of hearing cases referred up from lower courts.

James Madison refers to "the happiness of the people" to be the highest purpose of the proposed Constitution. **As I wrote in Part Two, defenders of the above rulings, as well as those rulings on possession of firearms, turn the purposes of the Constitution on its head. These arguments mean that we, as a nation, are required to harm ourselves— allow elections to be decided by money; create a permanent lower class** citizenship leading to all kinds of social pathology; allow anyone to go anywhere carrying a gun, often with the intent of looking for an excuse to use it. A far cry from, "the happiness of the people."

Do any of us think that unlimited spending by millionaires and billionaires and billion-asset corporations to political campaigns is compatible with our government deriving its just powers from the "consent of the governed?" Do any of us think that gerrymandering to carve out safe areas for certain candidates is providing for "the consent of the governed?" Do any of us think that when a government devises voting rules to purposely exclude or discourage certain classes of US citizens from voting that that government "derives its just powers from the consent of the **governed?**" Yet, our courts, executive, and legislative bodies build and protect these practices.

In *Federalist Paper Number 78, Hamilton* goes on, "For I agree that 'there is no liberty, if the power of the judging be not separated from the legislative and executive powers.'" … "The complete independence of the courts of justice is peculiarly essential in a limited Constitution." … "There is no position which depends on clearer principles than that every act of a delegated authority, contrary to the tenor of the commission under which it is exercised, is void. No legislative act, therefore, contrary to the Constitution can be valid."… "The interpretation of the laws is the proper and peculiar province of the courts. A constitution is, in fact, and must be regarded by the judges, as a fundamental law. It therefore belongs to them to ascertain its meaning, as well as the meaning of any particular act proceeding from the legislative body. If there should happen to be an irreconcilable variance between the two, that which has the superior obligation and validity ought, of course, to be preferred; or in other words, the Constitution ought to be preferred to the statute, the intention of the people to the intention of their agents."

I will insert here; this puts a tremendous burden on the judges. If federal judges followed this rule, they would put aside their political viewpoints and rely on the meaning of the Constitution—the

Constitution as a whole. Is this within the realm of human possibility? **Yes.** Thousands of juries every day (made up of ordinary citizens) make findings based on the evidence. Is it asking too much for our august federal judges to put aside their political preferences and perform their constitutional obligations?

In *Federalist Paper Number 80 Hamilton* writes, "In the first place, there is not a syllable in the plan under consideration which directly empowers the national courts to construe the laws according the spirit of the Constitution, or which gives them any greater latitude in this respect than may be claimed by the courts of every State, I admit, however, that the Constitution ought to be the standard of construction for the laws, and that wherever there is an evident opposition, the laws ought to give place to the Constitution. But this doctrine is not deducible from any circumstance peculiar to the plan of the convention, but from the general theory of a limited Constitution; and as far as it is true, is equally applicable to most, of not to all the State governments. There can be no objection, therefore, on this account, to the federal judicature which will not lie against the local judicatures in general, and which will not serve to condemn every constitution that attempts to set bounds to legislative discretion."

This would be fine if the Supreme Court, were truly a court sitting in a solemn fashion to dispassionately interpret the Constitution and not a group of nine persons dressed in black robes acting as a **legislature of last resort**.

In *Federalist Paper Number 81, Hamilton* writes: "It may be in the last place be observed that the supposed danger of judiciary encroachments on the legislative authority, which has been upon may occasions reiterated, is in reality contraventions of the will of the legislature may now and then happen, but they can never be so extensive as to amount to an inconvenience, or in any sensible degree to affect the order of the political system. This may be inferred with certainty from the general nature which it relates, from the manner in which it is

Darrel A Nash
94

exercised, from its comparative weakness, and from its total incapacity to support its usurpations by force. And the inference is greatly fortified by the consideration of the important constitutional check which the power of institution impeachments in one part of the legislative body [the House], and of determining upon them in the other [the Senate], would give to the body upon the members of the judicial department. This is alone a complete security. There never can be danger that the judges, by a series of deliberate usurpations on the authority of the legislature, would hazard the united resentment of the body intrusted with it, while this body was possessed of the means of punishing their presumption by degrading them from their stations. While this ought to remove all apprehensions on the subject, it affords, at the same time, a cogent argument for constituting the Senate a court for the trial of impeachments."

This paragraph is rather tortuous to follow and I am not sure what it is saying. Why bring into this paper the functions of the House and Senate in removing an official from office? However, the main reason the passage caught my attention is again arguing the relative powerlessness of the Court. Both political parties and many political partisans over recent decades have argued that the Supreme Court has overstepped its authority. Yet almost no legislative actions have been taken to reverse rulings in great contention. And the Court on occasion, like Citizens United, decides to take up cases and make rulings without requests for rulings from Congress or referrals of lower courts. Where is its powerlessness?

Federalist Paper Number 83 by *Hamilton* covers the issue of courts with emphasis on trials and whether and where the accused has the right to trial by jury. The author argues that the proposed constitution does not cover a lot of individual situations and that the various States have different courts and different systems. This raises the question of fairness and equal protection. A defendant in Mississippi usually cannot expect the same justice as one in Connecticut, for example.

The following, although written for the topic of courts and trials, probably applies to a lot of other issues considered in the Constitutional convention.

"From this sketch it appears that there is a material diversity, as well in the modification as in the extent of the institution of trial by jury in civil cases, in the several States; and from this fact these obvious reflections flow first, that no general rule could have been fixed upon by the convention which would have corresponded with the circumstances of all the States; and secondly, **that more or at least as much might have been hazarded by taking the system of any one State for a standard, as by omitting a provision altogether and leaving the matter as has been done, to legislative regulation.**" ... "It may be asked, why could not a reference have been made to the constitution of this State, taking that, which is allowed by me to be a good one, as a standard for the United States? I answer that it is not very probable the other States would entertain the same opinion of our institution as we do ourselves. It is natural to suppose that they are hitherto more attached to their own, and that each would struggle for the preference. If the plan of taking one State as a model for the whole had been thought of in the convention, it is to be presumed that the adoption of it in that body would have been rendered difficult by the predilection of each representation in favour of its own government; and it must be uncertain which of the States would have been taken as the model. And I leave it to conjecture whether under all circumstances, it is most likely that New York, or some other State, would have been preferred. **But admit that a judicious selection could have been effected in the convention, still there would have been great danger of jealousy and disgust in the other States at the partiality which had been shown to the institutions of one. The enemies of the plan would have been furnished with a fine pretext for raising a host of local prejudices against it, which perhaps might have hazarded, in no inconsiderable degree, it final establishment.**

So he is saying that compromises were made in order to get to sufficient agreement for a proposed Constitution that had a chance of being ratified. This is quite different from arguing, as some moderns do, that the Constitution is some sacrosanct document—that is has found the way forward that is not to be meddled with.

Before leaving the topic and the judicial system and relating back to the comments on The Federalist Society, here are excerpts from <u>The New Yorker</u>.

The article asks where Supreme Court Justices go to get their opinions. [The article answers, wherever they can find a justification for their position]

"Generally, appeals to tradition provide little relief for people who, historically, have been treated unfairly by the law. You can't fight segregation, say, by an appeal to tradition; segregation was an entrenched American tradition."

"In 1857, in Dred Scott, the Supreme Court asked whether any "negro whose ancestors were imported into this country and sold as slaves" is "entitled to all the rights, privileges, and immunities" guaranteed in the Constitution. Relying on "historical facts" the Court answered no, arguing that, at the time of the framing, black people "had for more than a century before been regarded as being of an inferior order, and all together unfit to associate with the white race either in social or political relations, and so far inferior that they had no rights which the white man was bound to respect."

"In 1896, Plessy v. Ferguson, essentially reprising Dred, cited the "established usages, customs, and traditions of the people "in affirming the constitutionality of Jim Crow laws."

"Originalism is essentially a very tightly defined history test. Snyder's invocation of "the traditions and conscience of our people" is like a readers pass to the library stacks. There is virtually no end of places in the historical record to look for the traditions and conscience of one people, especially when "our people" is everyone. Originalism, a term coined in 1980, asks judges to read only the books on a single shelf in the library; the writings of delegates to the Constitutional Convention and the ratifying conventions, the Federalist Papers, and a handful of other newspapers and pamphlets published between 1787 and 1791 (and occasionally public records relating to debates over subsequent amendments, especially the Fourteenth)."

"In 1985, in a speech to the Federalist Society, Ronald Reagan's Attorney General, Edwin Meese, announced the "the Administration's approach to constitutional interpretation" was to be rooted in the text of the Constitution as illuminated by those who drafted, proposed, and ratified it." He called this a "jurisprudence or original intention," and contrasted it with the "misuse of history" by jurists who saw, in the Constitution "spirit," things like "concepts of human dignity" with which they had turned the Constitution into a "charter for judicial activism." Meese's statement met with a reply from Justice William Brennan, who said that anyone who had ever studied in the archives know better than to believe that the records of the Constitutional Convention and the ratifying conventions offered so certain, exact, and singular a verdict as that which Meese expected to find there. (Obama's Supreme Court nominee, Merrick B. Garland clerked for Brennan.) Brennan called the idea that modern judges could discern the framer's original intention, "little more than arrogance cloaked as humility." *Lepore, p. 66* Contrary to this modern interpretation, *Fischer* writes: "In the debates over the wording of the Ninth and Tenth Amendments, we also find clear evidence that most original framers of the Constitution and Bill of Rights were not themselves 'originalists.' By a vote of 32 to 17, they supported the idea that the interpretation of this great document should be open to growth and change in 'admitted powers by implication.' As James Madison himself puts it." *Labunski, editor's note by Fischer.*

THE UNITED STATES FOR WHITE MALE PROPERTY OWNERS

Let's look at *Federalist Paper Number 54*. This is one of the more difficult papers to comprehend so far. This makes me lean toward thinking that *Hamilton* is the author. I get the impression reading this Paper that the author did not necessarily subscribe to the arguments, but rather developed the Paper to assuage the fears of southern delegates that the Constitution would take away the power they had over the African and descendants of African captives.

"Slaves are considered as property, not as persons."

I didn't start reviewing the Papers with the issue of slavery in mind—but it is an astonishing—yes, sickening—treatise. It goes into the discussion of how to count slaves as a part of the population. The discussion compares how population should be counted and how wealth should be counted. Numbers of people and "direct taxes" shall be apportioned among the several states.

"All this is admitted, it will perhaps be said; but does it follow, from an admission of numbers for the measure of representation, or of slaves combined with free citizens as a ratio of taxation, that slaves ought to be included in the numerical rule of representation? Slaves are considered as property, not as persons. They ought therefore to be comprehended in estimates of taxation which are founded on property, and to be excluded from representation which is regulated by a census of persons. This is the objection, as I understand it, stated in its full force. I shall be equally candid in stating the reasoning which may be offered on the opposite side.

"We subscribe to the doctrine," might one of our Southern brethren observe, "that representation relates more immediately to persons, and taxation more immediately to property, and we join in the application of this distinction to the case of our slaves. But we must deny the fact that slaves are considered merely as property, and in no respect whatever as persons. The true state of the case is, that they partake of both these qualities: being considered by our laws, is some respects, as persons, and in other respects as property. In being compelled to labour, not for himself, but for a master; in being vendible by on master to another master; and in being subject at all times to be restrained in his liberty and chastised in his body, by the capricious will of another,—the slave may appear to be degraded from the human rank, and classed with those irrational animals which fall under the legal denomination property. In being protected, on the other hand, in his life and his limbs, against the violence of all others, even the master of his labour and his liberty; and in being punishable himself for all violence committed against others,—the slave is no less evidently regarded by the law as a member of the society, not as a part of the irrational creation; as a moral person, not as a mere article of property. The federal Constitution, therefore, decides with great propriety on the case of our slaves, when it views them in the mixed character of persons and of property. This is character of persons and of property. This is in fact, their true character. It is the character bestowed on them by the laws under which they live; and it will not be denied that these are the proper criterion; because it is only under the pretext that the laws have transformed the negroes into subjects of property that a place is disputed them in the computation of numbers; **and it is admitted, that if the laws were to restore the rights which have been taken away, the negroes could no longer be refused an equal share of representation with other inhabitants."**

"This question may be placed in another light. It is agreed on all sides, that numbers are the best scale of wealth and taxation, as they are the only proper scale of representation. Would the convention have been impartial or consistent, if they had rejected the slaves from the lists when the shares of were to be calculated, and inserted them on the lists when the tariff of contributions was to be adjusted? Could it be reasonably expected that the Southern States would concur in a system which considered their slaves in some degree as men when burdens were to be imposed but refused to consider them in the same light when advantages were to be conferred. Might not some surprise also be expressed, that those who reproach the Southern States with **the barbarous policy of considering as property a part of their human brethren**, should themselves contend that the government to which all the States are to be parties, ought to consider this unfortunate race more completely in the unnatural light of property than the very laws of which they complain?"

"It may be replied, perhaps, that slaves are not included in the estimate of representatives in any of the States possessing them. They neither vote themselves nor increase the votes of their masters. Upon what principle, then, ought they to be taken into the federal estimate of representation? In rejecting them altogether, the Constitution would, in this respect, have followed the very laws which have been appealed to as the proper guide."

"This objection is repelled by a single observation. It is a fundamental principle of the proposed Constitution, that as the aggregate number of representatives allotted to the several States is to be determined by a federal rule, founded on the aggregate number of inhabitants, so the right of choosing this allotted number in each State is to be exercised by such part of the inhabitants as the State itself may designate. The qualifications on which the right of suffrage depend are not, perhaps, the same in any two States. In some of the States the difference is very material. In every State, a certain proportion of inhabitants are deprived of this right by the constitution of the State, who will be included in the census by which the federal Constitution apportions the representatives. In this point of view the Southern States might retort the complaint, by insisting that the principle laid down by the convention required that no regard should be had to the policy of particular States toward their own inhabitants; and consequently, that the slaves, as inhabitants, should have been admitted into the census according to their full number, in like manner with other inhabitants, who, by the policy of other States, are not admitted to all the rights of citizens. A rigorous adherence, however, to this principle, is waived by those who would by gainers by it. All that they ask is that equal moderation by shown on the other side. Let the case of the slaves be considered, as it is in truth, a peculiar one. Let the compromising expedient of the Constitution be mutually adopted, which regards them as inhabitants, but as debased by servitude below the equal level of free inhabitants; which regards the *slave* as divested of two-fifths of the *man*." **Ugh!**

The Paper goes on to a more general topic—how shall property be represented? (The terms wealth and property are used interchangeably.)

"After all, may not another ground be taken on which this article of the Constitution will admit of a still more ready defence? We have hitherto proceeded on the idea that representation related to persons only, and not at all to property. But is it a just idea? **Government is instituted no less for protection of the property, than of the persons, of individuals. The one as well as the other, therefore, may be considered as represented by those who are charged with the government.** Upon this principle it is that in several of the States, and particularly in the State of New York, one branch of the government is intended more especially to be the guardian of property, and is accordingly elected by that part of the society which is most interested in this object of government. In the federal Constitution this policy does not prevail. The rights of property are committed in the same hands with the personal right. Some attention ought therefore, to be paid to property in the choice of those hands."

Commentary: The author seems to be saying, that persons with property ought to have an edge in being elected to office. Indeed, protection of property is an essential function of government. By giving special powers to property owners, however, it is difficult for property-less persons to move into the ranks of property owners and thus be eligible for public office. And protection of property should not only be given to that with lots of property, but for those with very little—a few acres of land, a mule, an ox, some household furnishings. These small property owners were the ones that participated in Shay's rebellion and various other rebellions around the time before and after the Constitution was drafted and ratified.

"For another reason, the votes allowed in the federal legislature to the people of each State ought to bear some proportion to the comparative wealth of the States. States have not, like individuals, an influence over each other, arising from superior advantages of fortune. If the law allows an opulent citizen but a single vote in the choice of his representative, the respect and consequence which he derives from his fortunate situation very frequently guide the votes of others to the objects of his choice; and through this imperceptible channel the rights of property are conveyed into the public representation."

So he is saying that the opulent citizen will be so respected by others that they will follow his lead in voting. In this way the "fortunate" man will get extra weight in selecting representatives.

All this is not just an idle political argument. The Constitution, before the 13th, 14th, and 15th amendments legitimized slavery. African captives and their descendants were assigned 3/5 of a person when counting the number of people in the dicentennial census for purposes of determining the number of Congressmen allowed for each State—while they themselves had no voting rights. So "we the people" didn't include those in chattel slavery. Chattel slavery was for those of African descent meaning that **they and their offspring were "owned"** by their captor in perpetuity and thus could be kept or sold at the owner's discretion. (Chattel is an old word for cattle.) Think about, if you can, what you may have felt like being defined this way if you were an African or a descendant of Africans, being held captive and forced into labor by your captor, and your children and lover subject to being sold off to someone else, that lives who knows where.

Likewise, "we the people" did not include other groups including indentured servants and Native Americans (Indigenous People, First People). If we have been sensitive at all to the history of the Indigenous People we know how the Americas were taken from them by European immigrants. From the viewpoint of the Indigenous People, Europeans were invaders. Until modern times, our First People had no citizenship rights.

Zinn, in <u>A People's History of the United States</u>, writes, "The problem of democracy in post-Revolutionary society was not, however, the Constitutional limitations on voting. It lay deeper, beyond the Constitution, in the division of society into rich and poor. For if some people had great wealth and great influence, of they had the land, the money, the newspapers, the church, the educational system—how could voting, however broad, cut into such power?" *Zinn, Chapter 5, p. 96.*

The following topic in *Federalist Paper Number 54* by *Hamilton* is confusing without further digging because the federal government was originally almost totally funded by tariffs. The argument leads a reader to think that "direct" or taxes based on the number of people was to be instituted with the ratifying of the Constitution. So the "counterbalancing" argument presented below is a little disingenuous—it refers to something that can be—not what is.

To understand what the discussion is about, I had to go elsewhere and found this. "The Constitution specifically limited Congress' ability to impose direct taxes, by requiring it to distribute direct taxes in proportion to each state's census population. It was thought that head taxes and property taxes (slaves could be taxed as either or both) were likely to be abused, and that they bore no relation to the activities in which the federal government had a legitimate interest. The fourth clause of Article 1, section 9 therefore specifies that, 'No Capitation, or other direct, Tax shall be laid, unless in Proportion to the Census or enumeration herein before directed to be taken.'" *Foster, pp. 415 - 423*

This now relates back to the issue of how slaves are to be counted in "imposing direct taxes." Thus, if a direct tax is to be imposed, it would be based on "in Proportion to the Census or enumeration herein before directed to be taken." So States would count the number of inhabitants, except that slaves would count as 3/5 of a person.

Paper 54 argues that with a direct tax, there is an incentive for States to puff up numbers of inhabitants when qualifying for the maximum number of representatives and an incentive to minimize the amount of wealth (including the value of slaves) when direct taxes would be imposed. These two incentives will counterbalance and result in States giving the right number.

Thusly, "In one respect, the establishment of a common measure for representation and taxation will have a very salutary effect. As the accuracy of the census to be obtained by the Congress will necessarily depend, in a considerable degree, on the disposition, if not on the operation, of the States, it is of great importance that the States should feel as little bias as possible to swell or to reduce the amount of their numbers. Were their share of representation alone to be governed by this rule, they would have an interest in exaggerating their inhabitants. Were the rule to decide their share of taxation alone, a contrary temptation would prevail. By extending the rule to both objects, the States will have opposite interests, which will control and balance each other, and produce the requisite impartiality."

So slaves are to be the instrument to keep the States honest!

The arguments here are important for another reason. As stated in STATES' RIGHTS above, other sources besides the Federalist Papers report intense disagreements, direct taxation being one. This further emphasizes that the Constitution is a result of major compromises. "As he [George Mason] would explain repeatedly to the delegates, Mason was especially incensed about the power of proposed government to tax citizens directly. For months the Anti-Federalists had been raising the prospect of aggressive federal tax collectors swooping down on vulnerable citizens to take from them whatever money the state tax authorities had left behind. He argued that the ability to lay direct taxes against the people would 'entirely change the confederation of the States into one consolidated government ...[which] is totally subversive of every principle which has hitherto governed us." *Labunski, pp. 82-83.*

Question: would changing the confederation of the States into one consolidated government be a bad thing? "One nation, indivisible…with liberty and justice for all …"

THE DOCTRINE OF DISCOVERY

Part of the history of the Americas that is not well-known is how it was, and still is to a large extent, that aborigines have no power or property rights. Here is how that came about. As Europeans were exploring and invading Africa and the Americas, Pope Nicholas V in 1455 issued a Papal Bull—a proclamation—called the Doctrine of Discovery. The Doctrine of Discovery is now a principle of international law. It … specifically sanctioned and promoted the conquest, colonization, and exploitation of non-Christian territories and peoples. Hundreds of years of decisions and laws continuing right up to our own time can ultimately be traced back to the Doctrine of Discovery—laws that invalidate or ignore the rights, sovereignty, and humanity of indigenous peoples in the United States and around the world.

"From the mid-fifteenth century to the mid-twentieth century, most of the non-European world was colonized under the Doctrine of Discovery, one of the first principles of international law Christian European monarchies promulgated to legitimize investigating, mapping, and claiming lands belonging to peoples outside Europe. It originate in a papal bull issued in 1455 that permitted the Portuguese monarchy to seize West Africa. Following Columbus's infamous exploratory voyage in 1492, sponsored by the king and queen of the infant Spanish state, another papal bull extended similar permission to Spain. Disputes between the Portuguese and Spanish monarchies led to the papal-initiated Treaty of Tordesillas (1494), which, besides dividing the globe equally between the two Iberian empires, clarified that only non-Christian lands fell under the discovery doctrine." (This source cites, Miller, "International Law of Colonization," See also, Deloria, *Of Utmost Good Faith*, 6-39; Newcomb, Pagans in a Promised Land.) *Dunbar-Ortiz, p. 199*

"This doctrine on which all European states relied thus originated with the arbitrary and unilateral establishment of the Iberian monarchies' exclusive rights under Christian canon law to colonize foreign peoples, and this right was later seized by other European monarchical colonizing projects. The French Republic used this legalistic instrument for nineteenth- and twentieth-century settler colonists' projects, as did the newly independent United States when it continued the colonization of North America begun by the British." *Dunbar-Ortiz, p. 199*

"In 1791, not long after the US founding, Secretary of State Thomas Jefferson claimed that the Doctrine of Discovery developed by European states was international law applicable to the new US government as well." *Dunbar-Ortiz, p. 199*

This Papal Bull stated that non-Christians had no rights and that whoever "discovered" a land had no obligation to respect or recognize any rights of non-Christians. This mentality certainly was used from the time of the first landings on the Caribbean and Gulf of Mexico shores and was continued by traders, explorers, cattlemen, pioneers, US Army, and settlers all the way to the West Coast. I have thought about the purchase of Louisiana (Louisiana Purchase) by the US from France. The US now "owned" the land. I have not seen any concern that the Indigenous People might think that they already owned the land. And, in fact, "In 1823, the United States Supreme Court issued its decision in Johnson v. M'Intosh. Writing for the majority, Chief John Marshall held that the Doctrine of Discovery had been as established principle of European law and of English law in effect in Britain's North American colonies and was also the law of the United States. The Court defined the exclusive property rights that a European country acquired by dint of discovery; 'Discovery gave title to the government, by whose subjects, or by whose authority, it was made, against all other governments, which title might be consummated by possession.' Therefore, European and Euro-American 'discoverers' had gained real-property rights in the lands of Indigenous peoples by merely planting a flag. Indigenous rights were, in the Court's words, 'in no instance, entirely disregarded; but were necessarily, to a considerable extent, impaired.' The Court further held that Indigenous 'rights to complete sovereignty, as independent nations, were necessarily diminished.' Indigenous people could continue to live on the land, but title resided with the discovering power, the United States. A later decision concluded that Native nations were 'domestic, dependent nations." *Dunbar-Ortiz, p. 199-200.*

"The Doctrine of Discovery is so taken for granted that it is rarely mentioned in historical or legal texts published in the Americas." *Dunbar-Ortiz, p. 200.*

Doctrine of Discovery – Recent History.

In 2012, the United Nations Economic and Social Council Permanent Forum on Indigenous Issues called for a mechanism to investigate historical land claims. *United Nations Economic and Social Council.*

During the General Convention of the Episcopal Church conducted from August 8 to 17, 2009, the bishops of the church adopted a resolution officially repudiating the discovery doctrine. *Schjonberg, Mary Frances*

At the 2012 Unitarian Universalist Association General Assembly in Phoenix, AZ, delegates of the Unitarian Universalist Association passed a resolution repudiating the Doctrine of Discovery and calling on Unitarian Universalists to study the Doctrine and eliminate its presence from the current-day policies, programs, theologies, and structures of Unitarian Universalism. *UUA Website*

In 2013, at its 29th General Synod, the United Church of Christ followed suit in repudiating the doctrine in a near-unanimous vote. *Weible, Diane*

At the 2016 Synod, 10-17 June in Grand Rapids, MI, delegates to the annual general assembly of the Christian Reformed Church rejected the Doctrine of Discovery as heresy in response to a study report on the topic. Synod is the annual general assembly of the Christian Reformed Church. *Van Farowe, Roxanne*

WHAT COULD HAVE BEEN

Who knows how our history would have turned out if the Constitution followed the vision of "we the people?" We know that except for the Preamble, it was an abomination for those without power. Slavery went on for another "four score and seven years,"—well, four score and nine years. Indigenous People were pushed from their lands by various means, all of which derived from the idea that they were less worthy than immigrants from Europe.

States, particularly the southern States took the rights given by the Constitution to further engrain the status of African captives and their descendants as not having basic human rights. Of course, this was not restricted to the south. New York and New England greatly benefited from slavery and often had great reservations about Lincoln's pursuit of the war and abolishing slavery.

I have wondered at times whether it was worth getting all 13 States to ratify the Constitution if the price was to allow chattel slavery to continue. Here is what one of the founders said.

George Mason, called "the father of the bill of rights" and a Virginia slaveholder, made some of the most fervent arguments in opposition to slavery. At the Constitutional Convention, August 22, 1787, his position is reported, "Slavery discourages arts and manufactures. The poor despise labor when performed by slaves. They prevent the immigration of Whites, who really enrich and strengthen a country. They produce the most pernicious effect on manners. Every master of slaves is born a tyrant. They bring the judgement of Heaven on a Country. As nations can not be rewarded or punished in the next world they must be in this. By an inevitable chain of causes and effects providence punishes national sins, by national calamities. He lamented that some of our Eastern brethren had embarked in the nefarious traffic. As to the States being in possession of the Right to import, this was the case with many other rights, now to be properly given up. He held it essential in every point of view that the General Government should have power to prevent the increase of slavery." *Kaminski, p. 59.*

Mason, said in his address to the Virginia Ratifying Convention, "The augmentation of slaves weakens the States; and such a trade is diabolical in itself, and disgraceful to mankind. ... As much as I value an union of all the States, I would not admit the southern States into the Union, unless they agreed to the discontinuance of this disgraceful trade, because it would bring weakness and not strength to the Union." *Kaminski, p. 186, 187*

Comment. These arguments show the ambivalence of several of the Founders. Mason was a large holder in captivity of Africans and African descendants in Fairfax County, second only to George Washington. The argument made at the Virginia Convention was a part of the effort of Patrick Henry and George Mason to "raise doubts in the minds of convention delegates about the advisability of adopting the Constitution." *Kaminski, p. 185.* But I like his opposition to "this disgraceful trade."

As covered in Part One, the framers had to deal with jealously guarded powers of the States. They had a considerable amount of power under the Articles of Confederation, apparently reacting to the system they were under before independence from Britain was achieved. So a lot of powers were left to the States under the Constitution. The framers seemed to justify this by assuming that, contrary to what the federal government may do, the States would act for the benefit of **the people**. We see what this got us. "The people" were apparently property-owning males of northern European ancestry. For example, Rutledge of South Carolina said **the people** of North Carolina, South Carolina, and Georgia will never agree to this plan (the prohibition of importing Africans for enslavement after 20 years). (see the Anti-Federalist Papers, p. 165). No doubt Rutledge wasn't including those enslaved when he referred to, **"the people."**

The debates and ultimately the compromises made to propose and ratify the Constitution had two camps, 1) those that wanted only minimal adjustments to the Articles of Confederation so that the States retained substantial sovereignty—generally the southern States, and 2) those that saw that need for a more powerful Federal government to deal with foreign powers and the regulation of commerce among the States—generally northern States. A third possible interest group, or more accurately many interest groups, not a part of the debates and discussions, would be those at the margins of society who needed protection from power groups who could decide the livelihoods, freedoms, and general welfare of people who did not have political power.

Think about those who 1) worked in Ben Franklin's print shops, 2) those who worked on George Washington's, Thomas Jefferson's and George Masons' plantations, 3) indentured servants, 4) those who worked in Alexander Hamilton's businesses.

What kind of government would such groups have pushed for? If I was living in 1789 and had the station in life that I have now—white, male, property owner—I would have been in the 20 percent that could vote. So I can only guess at what those in the 80 percent would have pushed for if they had the right to vote. Here are some guesses; the right for all adult citizens to vote? Freedom from being captives and forced labor? Protection against beatings and worse from employers and slaveholders? The right to have to work no more than a reasonable number of hours each day and week? The right to equal power between debtors and debt-holders? Renters having some rights as to the terms of the rental agreement? The right to work in a safe workplace? The right to a decent pay for their work? The right to keep the land which they and their ancestors considered theirs? The right to give up land for a just compensation? The right to live their lives without government rules governing their life choices? The right to really have religious freedom—respect for non-Christian religious observances and practices? Equal power when it comes to contract law? See Shays Rebellion in *Zinn*, *pp. 93, 94, etc.*

I have been puzzled by the construction of *Federalist Paper Number 45* by *Madison*, already quoted extensively here.

He States that, "The powers delegated by the proposed constitution to the federal government are few and defined. Those which remain with the State governments are numerous and indefinite." He writes as if this settles the matter.

However, these sentences follow (with some paragraphs between) from a long discourse by Madison, that I have noted that for me is the most eloquent statement of why we have our government.

"…We have heard of the impious doctrine of the Old World, that the people were made for kings, not kings for the people. Is the same doctrine not to be revived in the New in a different shape—that the solid happiness of the people is to be sacrificed to the laws of political institutions of a different form? It is too early for politicians to presume on our forgetting that **the public good, the real welfare of the great body of people, is the supreme object to be pursued, and that no form of government whatever has any other value than as it may be fitted for the attainment of this object.** Were the plan of the convention adverse to the public happiness, my voice would be, Reject the plan. Were the Union itself inconsistent with the public happiness, it would be Abolish the Union. **In like manner, as far as the sovereignty of the States cannot be reconciled to the happiness of the people, the voice of every good citizen must be, Let the former be sacrificed to the latter.** How far the sacrifice is necessary has been shown. How far the unsacrificed residue will be endangered, is the question before us."

The first statement is dogmatic, the second pragmatic. Now read this—I may have discovered the disconnect.

In a study of the Constitution Convention by Stewart, we find the following. "The Convention adjourned from July 26 to August 6 to await the report of the <u>Committee of Detail</u>, which was to produce a first draft of the Constitution. It was chaired by <u>John Rutledge [Sorth Carolina]</u>, with the other members including <u>Edmund Randolph [Virginia]</u>, <u>Oliver</u>

Ellsworth [Connecticut], James Wilson [Pennsylvania], and Nathaniel Gorham [Massachusetts]."

"Much of what was included in the committee's report consisted of numerous details that the Convention had never discussed but which the committee correctly viewed as uncontroversial and unlikely to be challenged; and as such, much of the committee's proposal would ultimately be incorporated into the final version of the Constitution without debate." *Stewart, p. 165*

However, "[T]he five committee members ... added provisions that the Convention never discussed. They changed critical agreements that the delegates had already approved. Spurred by Rutledge, they reconceived the powers of the federal government, redefined the powers of the states, and adopted fresh concessions on the most explosive issue, slavery. It is not too much to say that Rutledge and his committee hijacked the Constitution, then remade it." *Stewart, p. 165*

"Three of the Rutledge Committee's changes fundamentally reconstituted the new government. Two dealt with the core problem of how to balance power between the states and the national government, though those transformations prompted no dissent from other delegates. The third tore open the divide between North and South." *Stewart, p. 170* "Though Rutledge wanted a stronger national government, he had no interest in an all-powerful one. He insisted that only specific powers should be assigned to the new government. **Edmund Randolph responded ... that Congress's powers could not be defined better, a contention Wilson echoed.**" *Stewart, p. 170*

"In mid-July, Rutledge again demanded a "specification of the powers" for Congress. Randolph now agreed with him.

"The committee did not waste time modifying the broad language approved by the Convention just two weeks before. Randolph's outline ignored that provision with eighteen "enumerated power, many drawn from the Articles of Confederation. Those eighteen powers began with the power to impose taxes, continued through making war, and finished with declaring what constitutes treason. **By this transformation, the committee made the new national government one of limited powers, and did so without any indication that the Convention desired the change.**" *Stewart, p. 170 & 171.*

So back to *Madison* in Federalist Paper Number 45. Often called the father of the Constitution, Madison I am sure, was determined to see it ratified. Faced with the draft that came out from Rutledge's revisions, he had to argue for it as published. I have a strong feeling that Federalist Paper Number 45 and other of his Federalist Papers starts with where his heart was and later transform to where his head is—to get the Constitution ratified. **Now who do we say is the father of the Constitution?**

It seems that the Constitution we have is to a considerable degree, a result of exhaustion of many of the delegates.

The Bill of Rights. In *Federalist Paper Number 84, Hamilton* argues against including a bill of rights in the Constitution. His wording is a premonition of the twisted arguments we get into today—free speech, paying for elections, right for everyone to carry a gun around, etc.

"**I further and affirm that bills of rights, in the sense and to the extent in which they are contended for, are not only unnecessary in the proposed Constitution, but would even be dangerous.** They would contain various exceptions to powers not granted; and on this very account, would afford a colourable pretext to claim more than were granted." See esp. the Second Amendment. "For why declare that things shall not be done which there is not power to do? Why, for instance, should it be said that the liberty of the press shall not be restrained when no power is given by which restrictions may be imposed? I will not contend that such a provision would confer a regulating power; but it is evident that it would furnish, to men disposed to usurp, a plausible pretence for claiming that power. They might urge with a semblance of reason that the Constitution ought not to be charged with the absurdity of providing against the abuse of an authority which was not given, and that the provision against restraining the liberty of the press afforded a clear implication that a power to prescribe proper regulations concerning it was intended to be vested in the national government. This may serve as a specimen of the number handles which would be given to the doctrine of constructive powers by the indulgence of an injudicious zeal for bills of rights."

Hamilton's arguments against having a bill of rights, if he had won, may have saved as from the follies visited on us, one of insisting, based on the First Amendment that we are forced to let money buy elections (corporations are people) and two, the Second Amendment, which is used to justify letting anyone at any time, carry and use firearms.

WHAT HAS HAPPENED

The topic of taxes in *Federalist Paper Number 54* by *Hamilton* is confusing without further digging because the federal government was originally almost totally funded by tariffs. The argument leads a reader to think that "direct taxes" or taxes based on the number of people was to be instituted with the ratifying of the Constitution. So the "counterbalancing" argument presented below is a little disingenuous— it refers to something that can be—not what is.

I have to go back to an earlier part of *Paper 54*—covered above—on the matter of how wealth may affect representation. "A State possesses no such influence over other States. It is not probable that the richest State in the Confederacy will ever influence the choice of a single representative in any other State. Nor will the representatives of the larger and richer States possess any other advantage in the federal legislature, over the representatives of other States, than what may result from their superior numbers alone. As far, therefore, as their superior wealth and weight may justly entitle them to any advantage, it ought to be secured to them by a superior share of representation."

This is an optimistic argument. Fast forward to today. While "States" are constrained in this by the proposed Constitution, wealth in the form of campaign contributions is not constrained within a state. A rich citizen of Mississippi can influence who gets elected in New York or Connecticut. And now, you don't even have to be a citizen or a living breathing person to purchase representatives.

The means of maintaining "a proper responsibility to the people," has not worked because only a select portion of the population is franchised. A broader electorate who believed their vote would make a difference would be more likely to weed out the people this Paper said would be weeded out.

But, of course, the twin evils of gerrymandering and vast spending on elections by a small proportion of citizens greatly diminishes the voice of an individual seeking to remove an official subject to "degeneracy" while in office.

One might think that the issue of voter enfranchisement was settled by the Fourteenth Amendment, Section 1—"all persons born or naturalized in the United States, and subject to the jurisdiction thereof, are citizens of the United States and of the State wherein they reside. No State shall make or enforce any law which shall abridge the privileges or immunities of citizens of the United States; nor shall any State deprive any person of life, liberty, or property, without due process of law; not deny to any person within it jurisdiction the equal protection of the laws."

Who was left to be enfranchised, not covered in this amendment? How was this amendment enforced between 1865 and 1965?

Zinn, in the citation above, provides a more general criticism of the Constitution. He says that reducing and managing conflicts among the "factions" is an objective of those who are in power. "**But is it the aim of government simply to maintain order as a referee, between two equally matched fighters? Or is it that government has some special interest in maintaining a certain kind of order, a certain distribution**

of power and wealth, a distribution of which government officials are not neutral referees, but participants? In that case, the disorder of which they might worry about is the disorder of popular rebellion against those monopolizing the society's wealth."

"When economic interest is seen behind the political clauses of the Constitution, then the document becomes not simply the work of wise men trying to establish a decent and orderly society, but the work of certain groups trying to maintain their privileges, while giving just enough rights and liberties to the people to ensure popular support." *Zinn p. 97.*

A reader of the following paragraphs, without digging into who may be an elector can easily be convinced of a great democracy to be instituted by the Constitution. An adult reading this Paper at the time might justifiably believe that he now has the right to vote or to become a candidate for office.

From *Federalist Paper Number 57, Hamilton or Madison* we get, "Who are to be the electors of the federal representatives? Not the rich, more than the poor, not the learned, more than the ignorant, not the haughty heirs of distinguished names, more that the humble sons of obscurity and unpropitious fortune. The electors are to be the great body of the people of the United States. They are to be the same who exercise the right in every state of electing the corresponding branch of legislature of the State."

"Who are the objects of popular choice? Every citizen whose merit may recommend him to the esteem and confidence of his country. No qualification of wealth, of birth, of religious faith, or of civil profession is permitted to fetter the judgement or disappoint the inclination of the people."

One can imagine that if a proponent of the proposed Constitution were speaking, he would hurriedly and maybe in a mumbling voice say that everyone can vote for a congressman that possesses the right to vote for state representative. The speaker would hope no one asks about enfranchisement at the State level. Recall in Part One the review of State constitutions around the time of ratifying the US Constitution in almost all cases, restricted qualified voters to white male property owners.

Federalist Paper Number 57 goes on to discuss the construction of the Senate.

"In this spirit it may be remarked, that the equal vote allowed to each State is at once a constitutional recognition of the portion of sovereignty remaining in the individual States, and an instrument for preserving that residuary sovereignty. So far the quality ought to be no less acceptable to the large than to the small States; since they are not less solicitous to guard, by every possible expedient, against an improper consolidation of the States into one simple republic."

There is a presumption, without analysis that "consolidation of the States into one simple republic" is a bad thing. Nor is this a simple either/or. There can be other arrangements of geographic units to the federal government. Canada has provinces, which I presume, have fewer powers than our States.

"*Secondly.* The necessity of a senate is **not less indicated by the propensity of all single and numerous assemblies to yield to the impulse of sudden and violent passions, and to be seduced by factious leaders into intemperate and pernicious resolutions.**"

I am reading the above sentence on May 6, 2017, two days after the US House of Representatives passed by one vote to replace Obamacare with a Republican version that will make matters worse than before Obamacare. The bill was passed without most congresspersons reading it, without the Congressional Budget Office evaluating it, and contrary to commitments several Congresspersons had made to their constituents. It takes away many of the provisions that low income people had in order to get insurance, and provides huge savings to persons with income over $200,000. Hopefully, the Senate will do its duty as the author of this Paper anticipated.

The rest of *Paper Number 62 Hamilton or Madison*, is well worth reading. It is a condemnation—in advance—of the Trump Administration.

INTERNATIONAL TREATIES AND PRESIDENTIAL POWERS

John Jay in *Federalist Paper Number 64* argues for and strongly defends the provisions in the proposed Constitution for the making of international treaties by the president and with the advice and consent of the Senate.

"As the States are equally represented in the Senate, and by men the most able and the most willing to promote the interests of their constituents, they will all have an equal degree of influence in that body, especially while they continue to be careful in appointing proper persons, and to insist on their punctual attendance. **In proportion as the United States assume a national form and a national character, so will the good of the whole be more and more an object of attention, and the government must be a weak one indeed if it should forget that the good of the whole can only be promoted by advancing the good of each of the parts or members which compose the whole.** It will not be in the power of the President and Senate to make any treaties by which they and their families and estates will not be equally bound and affected with the rest of the community; and, **having no private interests distinct from that of the nation, they will be under no temptations to neglect the latter.**" Mr. Trump take notice. This argument is weakened, just as the one above, by the way we now choose our national representatives—gerrymandering and money, not people—determines who are representatives are.

Further, one of the tenets in constructing the US Constitution was that men will, if not checked, take all kinds of actions against the interests of citizens. That's why the Framers devised the system of "checks and balances." In the above, Jay is saying that this august body, filled "by men the most able and the most willing to promote the interests of their constituents," will do the right thing. If what Jay says is true, why put so much emphasis on checks and balances?

In *Federalist Paper Number 75 Hamilton* deals with making treaties with foreign governments and argues for the provisions in the proposed Constitution for the making of treaties by the president after receiving two-thirds of the senators' present concurrence.

There is a discourse on how the president might abuse this power and includes the following, which struck me, given the questions about foreign entanglements of Donald Trump.

"However proper or safe it may be in governments where the executive magistrate is an hereditary monarch, to commit to him the entire power of making treaties, it would be utterly unsafe and improper to intrust that power to an elective magistrate of four years' duration. … But a man raised from the station of a private citizen to the rank of chief magistrate, possessed of a moderate or slender fortune, and looking forward to a period not very remote when he may probably be obliged to return to the station from which he was taken, might sometimes be under temptations to sacrifice his duty to his interest, which it would require superlative virtue to withstand. An avaricious man might be tempted to **betray the interests of the state to the acquisition of wealth. An ambitious man might make his own aggrandizement, by the aid of a foreign power, the price of his treachery to his constituents.** The history of human conduct does not warrant that exalted opinion of human virtue which could make it wise in a nation to commit interests of so delicate and momentous a kind, as those which concern its intercourse with the rest of the world, to the sole disposal of a magistrate created and circumstanced as would be a President of the United States."

Hamilton has it backward on who would most likely be the "avaricious man." It is more likely that, the more a person possesses, the more likely he or she is to want to get more. Is Hamilton arguing that only rich men should be president? Later in the Paper, he expresses another confidence that is not always warranted.

"And whoever has maturely weighed the circumstances which must concur in the appointment of a President, will be satisfied that the office will always bid fair to be filled by men of such characters as to render their concurrence in the formation of treaties peculiarly desirable, as well on the score of wisdom, as on that of integrity." Oh, okay. This leads directly into the issue of the Electoral College.

THE ELECTORAL COLLEGE

Federalist Paper Number 68 and the Electoral College. As I am writing this, December 13, 2016, the country is in the throes of presidential succession. During the presidential campaign, many many persons in and out of government listened to and watched Donald Trump and concluded that by any measure or kind of qualification for this office, Trump is unfit to serve. In addition, both before and after the election, he has said and acted in many ways that show he is likely to have a chummy relationship with Russian president, Vladimir Putin and other world autocrats. Now it comes out that Putin acted directly in an effort to get Trump elected.

This situation has directed a lot of attention to what are the responsibilities of the Electoral College, especially since Trump did not receive the majority of the popular vote.

I have been wrestling with the question of whether the Electors are free to cast their vote on the basis of what they themselves view as whether Trump is unfit for office, especially his close relationship with Putin, who has been at war with the United States since Russia's invasion and occupation of Crimea—and I think years before that when he invaded the country of Georgia. Just as important, Trump's disregard and trashing a lot of the government institutions that have been developed over the years—in recent days it is the CIA.

It is almost certain that Trump will be certified as winning the election on December 19. And most likely, this will happen because of what I have already identified as a defect of the US Constitution—it is a States' rights Constitution, not a "we the people" constitution. A people's constitution, would set forth the requirements of the Electors for all States. **If the purpose of the Electoral College is as described in Federalist Paper 68, then the Electors would have to take into account whether Trump was qualified and whether he is likely to put the interests of foreign powers ahead of those of the United States.**

By the traditional way the Electoral College has voted in most elections, Trump will receive enough to be named president on December 19. However, Hillary Clinton received more popular votes, by some 2.7 to 2.8 million votes. Article Two of the US Constitution States that "Each State shall appoint, in such manner as **the legislature thereof may direct**, a number of electors, equal to the whole number of Senators and Representatives to which the State may be entitled to in the Congress; but no Senator or Representative, or person holding an office of trust or profit under the United States shall be appointed an elector."

As written now, Article Twelve of the Constitution governs how the president is chosen. "… the person having the greatest number of votes for President shall be the President if such number be a majority of the whole number of Electors appointed…"

From the following, we see that States have taken the Constitution into their own hands. "All states except California (before 1913), Maine, and Nebraska have chosen electors on a "winner-take-all" basis since the 1880s. *Morris, p. 67.* Under the winner-take-all system, the state's electors are awarded to the candidate with the most votes in that state, thus maximizing the state's influence in the national election. Maine and Nebraska use the "congressional district method", selecting one elector within each congressional district by popular vote and awarding two electors by a statewide popular vote. *History.com Staff.*

So, if 50.001 % of the popular vote of a state is for a certain candidate, then all of the Electoral votes go for that candidate. Following that, Trump will get more than 270 votes and will be declared the winner and our next president.

This is not how the Founders intended for the Electoral College to operate.

In *Federalist Paper Number 68, Hamilton* writes:

"Nothing was more to be desired than that every practicable obstacle should be opposed to cabal, intrigue, and corruption. These most deadly adversaries of republican government might naturally have been expected to make their approaches from more than one quarter, but **chiefly from the desire of foreign powers to gain an improper ascendant in our councils.** How could they better gratify this than by raising a creature of their own to the chief magistracy of the Union?"

"It was desirable that the sense of the people should operate in the choice of the person to whom so important a trust was to be confided. This end will be answered by committing the right of making it, not to any pre-established body, **but to men chosen by the people for the special purpose, and at the particular juncture.**"

"It was also peculiarly desirable to afford as little opportunity as possible to tumult and disorder. This evil was not least to be dreaded in the election of a magistrate*, who was to have so important an agency in the administration of the government as the President of the United States." *Magistrate refers to any public official. So the president is the chief magistrate of the US.

Hamilton goes on to say that the Electoral College will protect against this because the electors "have not made the appointment of the President to depend on any pre-existing bodies of men, who might be tampered with beforehand to prostitute their votes; but they have referred it in the first instant to an immediate act of the people of America, to be exerted in the choice of persons for the temporary and sole purpose of making the appointment." I interpret what he wrote to mean that the

Electoral College is to be made up of citizens who do not hold public office.

He perhaps is overly optimistic that those chosen as the Electors will not be "tampered with beforehand to prostitute their votes." "The process of election affords a moral certainty **that the office of President will never fall to the lot of any man who it not in an eminent degree endowed with the requisite qualifications.**"

After writing the above, I have found that the States, in the views of the Founders, have violated the very foundation of the purpose of the Electoral College as described by Hamilton. "Alexander Hamilton described the framers' view of how electors would be chosen, "A small number of persons, selected by their fellow-citizens from the general mass, will be most likely to possess the information and discernment requisite to such complicated [tasks]." **The founders assumed this would take place district by district**. That plan was carried out by many states until the 1880s. **For example, in Massachusetts** in 1820, the rule stated "the people shall vote by ballot, on which shall be designated who is voted for as an Elector for the district." *Resolves of The General Court of the Commonwealth of Massachusetts, p. 245*

In other words, the people did not place the name of a candidate for a president on the ballot, instead they voted for their local elector, whom they trusted later to cast a responsible vote for president."

"Some states reasoned that the favorite presidential candidate among the people in their state would have a much better chance if all of the electors selected by their state were sure to vote the same way – a "general ticket" of electors pledged to a party candidate." *James Madison*

Once one state took that strategy, the others felt compelled to follow suit in order to compete for the strongest influence on the election.

"When James Madison and Hamilton, two of the most important architects of the Electoral College, saw this strategy being taken by some states, they protested strongly. **Madison and Hamilton both made it** clear this approach violated the spirit of the Constitution. According to Hamilton, the selection of the president should be "made by men most capable of analyzing the qualities adapted to the station [of president]." According to Hamilton, the electors were to analyze the list of potential presidents and select the best one. He also used the term "deliberate." Hamilton considered a pre-pledged elector to violate the spirit of Article II of the Constitution insofar as such electors could make no "analysis" nor could "deliberate" concerning the candidates. Madison agreed entirely, saying that when the Constitution was written, all of its authors assumed individual electors would be elected in their districts and it was inconceivable a "general ticket" of electors dictated by a state would supplant the concept. In 1823, Madison wrote to George Hay, "explaining his views of the Electoral College, his strong opposition to states voting as winner-take-all blocs and his view of the origins of the winner-take-all rule. In addition to disenfranchising districts that voted against the preference of the state, Madison worried that statewide voting would increase sectionalism and the strength of geographic parties. He wrote that his views were widely shared by others at the Constitutional Convention, and that the winner-take-all approach had been forced on many states due to its adoption in other states: "The district mode was mostly, if not exclusively in view when the Constitution was framed and adopted; & was exchanged for the general ticket [e.g., winner-take-all rule] & the legislative election, as the only expedient for baffling the policy of the particular States which had set the example." *FairVote, Why James Madison Wanted to Change the Way We Vote For President*

"Madison and Hamilton were so upset by what they saw as a distortion of the framers' original intent that they advocated for a constitutional amendment to prevent anything other than the district plan: "the election of Presidential Electors by districts, is an amendment very proper to be brought forward", Madison wrote to George Hay in 1823, "The present rule of voting for President by the H. of Reps. is so great a departure from the Republican principle of numerical equality, and even from the federal rule which qualifies the numerical by a State equality, and is so pregnant also with a mischievous tendency in practice, that an amendment of the Constitution on this point is justly called for by all its considerate & best friends." *McCarthy, June 12, 2012.*

Hamilton went further. He actually drafted an amendment to the Constitution mandating the district plan for selecting electors.

Although the following document does not name Hamilton, I presume that he was instrumental in persuading the State of New York to propose the amendment. "1st. That Congress shall from time to time divide each State into Districts equal to the whole number of Senators and Representatives from such state in the Congress of the United States, and shall direct the mode of choosing an Elector of President and Vice President in each of the said Districts, who shall be chosen by Citizens who have the qualifications requisite for Electors of the most numerous branch of the State Legislature, and that the districts shall be formed, as nearly as may be, with an equal proportion of population in each, and of Counties and, if necessary, parts of Counties contiguous to each other, except when there may be any detached portion of territory not sufficient of itself to form a District which then shall be annexed to some other part nearest thereto." *Legislature of New York,* January 29, 1802

The Electoral College is now **voluntary party lackeys and intellectual non-entities**. This is serious. This is how we got Trump. After reading this, I am angry at our political commentators, editorial writers, politicians, educators, etc. for not making a big deal of how the Electoral College now disenfranchises US citizens. The public is largely in the dark. Perhaps this is of our own doing, after all, anyone with a computer can read Wikipedia or many other on-line sources. Or we could go to any well-stocked public library. Unfortunately, this is not how most of us get educated.

From what I understand, the current system has been found constitutional by the Supreme Court.

"However, even if such promises of candidates for the electoral college are legally unenforceable because violative of an assumed constitutional freedom of the elector under the Constitution, Art. II, § 1, to vote as he may choose in the electoral college, it would not follow that the requirement of a pledge in the primary is unconstitutional. A candidacy in the primary is a voluntary act of the applicant. He is not barred, discriminatorily, from participating but must comply with the rules of the party. Surely one may voluntarily assume obligations to vote for a certain candidate. The state offers him opportunity to become a candidate for elector on his own terms, although he must file his declaration before the primary. Code of Ala., Tit. 17, § 145. Even though the victory of an independent candidate for elector in Alabama cannot be anticipated the state does offer the opportunity for the development of other strong political organizations where the need is felt for them by a sizable block of voters. Such parties may leave their electors to their own choice."

"We conclude that the Twelfth Amendment does not bar a political party from requiring the pledge to support the nominees of the National Convention. Where a state authorizes a party to choose its nominees for elector in a party primary and to fix the qualifications for the candidates, we see no federal constitutional objection to the requirement of this pledge." *Supreme Court of the United States*

With the present system, why go to the bother of having an Electoral College? Just have a State official, such as the governor or secretary of state, duly verify the popular vote of her or his State and report the winner to the US Congress. That State would, as now, then be credited with votes equal to the number of US Representatives, plus the two US Senators.

In my experience, the voters have no idea who the members of the Electoral College are. All we know—and this is without verification—that they do not hold elective office. In Maryland—and I suppose all states—the public has no say in who is to serve on the Electoral College.

Hamilton says these persons, are chosen "for the temporary and sole purpose of making the appointment." How else are these Electors to be chosen than by being voted in "by the people?"

So here is how electors are chosen. Did you know? "Today, political parties usually nominate their slate of electors at their state conventions or by a vote of the party's central committee, with party loyalists often being picked for the job." *History.com, Staff*

I have no idea who served on the Electoral College for Maryland in 2016, nor in my memory and previous election. If the expectations of Hamilton and Madison had been carried out, candidates for the Electoral College would be on the ballot. Further, I presume, again in the expectations of the Founders, these candidates would make their case for their election on the basis of their "capability of analyzing the qualities adapted to the station of president" in Hamilton's words.

Under Hamilton's description of these Electors, they have a most solemn and difficult obligation—they must protect against "these most deadly adversaries of republican government [that] might naturally have been expected to make their approaches from more than one quarter, but **chiefly from the desire of foreign powers to gain an improper ascendant in our councils**. If the Electoral College worked in 2016 the way the Founders intended, they would consider, among other questions, whether a candidate is found wanting in unquestioned dedication to the United States and our Constitution. Trump would not have been chosen.

A columnist for the Washington Post, Charles Lane wrote an article December 15, 2016 admonishing us that we should get over the provision that the Electoral College elects the president. I regret that I didn't save his article, but the essence is that he made an analogy with the NFL. He said something like we don't get to change the way game winners are decided just because we don't like the result. His example was that we don't' get to make the winner to be the team that makes the most yardage. Here is my response.

Letter sent to Charles Lane, columnist for the Washington Post, December 15, 2016

Dear Mr. Lane:

About your article in the Post today, "We need to get over the popular vote."

The future of our country is not equivalent to rules for a sports league. Whenever I see an appeal to analogies, it gets my attention. If an argument can't be made without analogies, then I look for its weaknesses.

There is a reason for the Electoral College. During the presidential campaign, many many persons in and out of government listened to and watched Donald Trump and concluded that by any measure or kind of qualification for this office, Trump is unfit to serve. In addition, both before and after the election, he has said and acted in many ways that show he is likely to have a chummy relationship with Russian president, Vladimir Putin and other world autocrats. Now it comes out that Putin worked directly on getting Trump elected. Trump denies this. The Electoral College has the responsibility for casting their votes for someone whom they can say without reservation will obey, preserve, and defend the Constitution of the United States.

I am sure that many people, as I do, want the Electors to select Mrs. Clinton. But other presidents have taken office without receiving the highest number of votes. In these cases, there has never been, in my lifetime, such sentiment to have the Electoral College overturn the usual process of choosing the president.

BTW, The NFL does not have a body equivalent to the Electoral College.

Darrel Nash

Note: at the time I wrote this letter, I was not aware that many state laws, as reviewed above, prevent Electoral College electors from performing their citizen duties as envisioned by Hamilton.

THE SECOND AMENDMENT TODAY

Rights claimed for unlimited possession of firearms is of fairly recent origin. Almost all politicians today say that under the Second Amendment, governments cannot infringe the right of individuals to bear arms. I think a lot of them say this for fear of the NRA. As covered in Part Two, the Federalist Papers do not show that the current interpretation is correct. And the wording of the Amendment obviously has resulted in various interpretations over the decades and centuries. So let's look at some recent history.

The NRA wasn't always so extreme. In fact, for the majority of its 141 year history, the organization backed gun regulation and rarely if ever claimed that regulations were unconstitutional.

"In 1934, the NRA formed its Legislative Affairs Division to update members with facts and analysis of upcoming bills, after the National Firearms Act of 1934 (NFA) became the first federal gun-control law passed in the U.S. Karl Frederick, NRA President in 1934, during congressional NFA hearings testified **"I have never believed in the general practice of carrying weapons. I seldom carry one. ... I do not believe in the general promiscuous toting of guns. I think it should be sharply restricted and only under licenses."*** The NRA supported the NFA along with the Gun

Control Act of 1968 (GCA), which together created a system to federally license gun dealers and established restrictions on particular categories and classes of firearms." *Jilani* (bold added)

"During the testimony, Congressman Clemon T. Dickinson of Missouri asked Frederick if he thought anything being debated was unconstitutional. Although Frederick replied that he thought firearm regulation was a state issue, he also said he had not "given it any study from that point of view" that regulating guns may be unconstitutional." "Frederick did caution against over-regulating weapons during his testimony, but as the transcript above demonstrates, did not oppose all new gun regulations." "The NRA also went on to support the Gun Control Act of 1968. In fact, then-president Harold W. Glassen testified that his organization had long supported "sensible" gun regulation (although he resisted what he believed to be overregulation)." *Jilani*

Would that we had that system today!

In recent decades, the National Rifle Association (NRA), the main gun lobby, has refused to consider any common sense gun reforms following several mass shootings. It has instead chosen to be the primary group working to block reforms.

What has changed since 1934? Have we discovered some words in the Constitution that nobody knew were there? Maybe other documents like the Federalist Papers or other papers from that time that nobody knew about? No, what has changed is an attitude—a new way of interpreting the Constitution. This is one of those cases of "judicial activism" that we hear so much about in modern times.

Continuing with *Jilani,* "But in 1977, things changed. NRA leadership had an internal revolt at its Cincinnati meeting that forced out individuals within the organization who wanted its primary purpose to be promoting sportsmanship and gun safety."

"Its new Executive Vice President Harlon Carter scorned the moderate views the NRA held in the past: Now someone says to me…,

"Yes, but we took positions back five or six years ago, and we made statements some years ago," […] any position we took back at that time is no good, it is not valid, and it is simply not relevant to the problem that we face today. The latest news release from NRA embraces a disastrous concept… that evil is imputed to the sale and delivery, the possession of a certain kind of firearm, entirely apart from the good or evil intent of the man who uses it and/or (2) the legitimate use of a handgun is limited to sporting use." *Jilani*

"Carter realigned the organization, and it began to aggressively challenge handgun bans and invoke the 2nd amendment to challenge gun laws in court. And to this day, the NRA has failed to support a single major piece of gun reform legislation." *Jilani*

Further emphasizing the recent status of the Second Amendment, "Chief Justice Burger—a rock-ribbed conservative appointed by Richard Nixon—articulated the consensus when he called the idea of individual gun rights in the Constitution a preposterous fraud."… "For 218 years, judges overwhelmingly concluded that the amendment authorized states to form militias, what we call the National Guard. Then, in 2008, the U. S. Supreme Court upended two centuries of precedent. In the case of *District of Columbia v. Heller*, an opinion written by Justice Antonin Scalia declared that the Constitution confers a right to own a gun for self-defense in the home. That's right: the Supreme Court found there to be an individual right to gun ownership just a few years ago." *Waldman. pp. xii and xiii.*

Those seeking an in-depth study of the Second Amendment, how it was formulated, possible meanings at the time of passage, and evolving interpretations over the decades and centuries are encouraged to read *Waldman* in its entirety.

FEDERAL AND STATE POWERS

In *Federalist Paper Number 46, Madison* makes his strongest case for why a limited federal government will be preferred by the people.

He uses terms like, "everyone knows" and "it has already been proven." The proof, however, is limited to his own previous arguments that I have found in many cases to be assertions without citing data or experience or logic to support them.

"Many considerations besides those suggested on a former occasion, seem to place it beyond doubt that the first and most natural attachment of the people will be to the government of their respective States. Into the administration of these a greater number of individuals will expect to rise. From the gifts of these a greater number of offices and emoluments will flow. By the superintending care of these all the more domestic and personal interests of the people will be regulated and provided for. With the affairs of these, the people will be more familiarly and minutely conversant. And with the member of these will a greater proportion of the people have the ties of personal acquaintance and friendship, and of family and party attachments, on the side of these, therefore, the popular bias my well be expected most strongly to incline."

This is certainly true and hardly needs stating. If you need the sewer fixed or streets repaired, it is beyond argument that a local government is the best to call, especially if you are on a first name basis with the official in charge.

But what about this—**Equal justice under law**—a phrase engraved on the front of the United States Supreme Court building. When it comes to matters of equity and justice, the states in many notable cases have failed miserably—especially during chattel slavery and the follow-up reign of terror. Should not the citizen of any State have the constitutional right to matters of equity and justice as any other?

Racism is the most egregious of actions done under the banner of States' Rights. But do citizens in all jurisdictions have the same rights to affordable and safe housing? Can someone accused of a crime expect the same justice regardless of the State he or she resides in? Why not, (see above phrase)? Do kids across all 50 states and in all jurisdictions have equal access to education? We know the answer. What about equal pay for equal work? Do workers in all states have the right to the same working conditions, hours of work, safe conditions, etc.? What about the freedom for adults to make life choices? It makes little sense that many businesses are regulated at the State level, like insurance. Why should people in one state have less protection against insurance company flim flam than those in another state?

Continuing with *Madison* in *Federalist Paper Number 46*, "Experience speaks the same language in this case. The federal administration, though hitherto vey defective in comparison with what may be hoped under a better system, had during the war, and particularly whilst the independent fund of paper emissions was in credit, and activity and importance as great as it can well have in any future circumstances whatever. It was engaged, too, on a course of measures which had for their object the protection of everything that could be desirable to the people at large. It was nevertheless, invariably found, after the transient enthusiasm for the early Congresses were over, that the attention and attachment of the people were turned anew to their own particular governments; that the federal council was at no time the idol of popular favour and *that opposition to proposed enlargements of its powers and importance was the side usually taken by the men who wished to build their political consequence on the prepossessions* of the fellow citizens.*"

*prepossessions; a prejudice, esp. one in favor of a person or thing. The Random House Dictionary of the English Language, 1967

I don't understand the italicized part of the sentence. Here is my attempt. 'Opposition to enlarging the federal government comes from those wanting to gain power based on the prejudices of fellow citizens.' I can't discern whether he thinks this is a good thing or not. And I don't understand the point of the phrase.

Now this. "If therefore, as has been elsewhere remarked, the people should in future become more partial to the federal than to the State governments, the change can only result from such manifest and irresistible proofs of a better administration, as will overcome all their antecedent propensities. And in that case, the people ought not surely to be precluded from giving most of their confidence where they may discover it to be most due; but even in the case the State governments could have little to apprehend, because it is only within a certain sphere that the federal power can, in the nature of things, be advantageously administered."

"So far as the disposition of each [State governments and the federal government] towards the other may be influenced by these causes, the State governments must clearly have the advantage. But in a distinct and very important point of view, the advantage will lie on the same side. The prepossessions, which the member themselves will carry into the federal government, will generally be favourable to the States; *whilst it will rarely happen that the members of the State governments will carry into the public councils a bias to favour of the general government.* A local spirit will infallibly prevail much more in the members of Congress that a national spirit will prevail in the legislatures of the particular States. Everyone knows that a great proportion of the errors committed by the State legislatures proceeds from the disposition of the members to sacrifice the comprehensive and permanent interest of the State, to the particular and separate views of the counties or districts in which they reside. And if they do not sufficiently enlarge their policy to embrace the collective welfare of the particular State, how can it be imagined that they will make the aggregate prosperity of the Union, and the dignity and respectability of its government, the objects of their affections and consultations?"

*This argument is a little weird. *"... whilst it will rarely happen..."* What kind of argument is this? What experience or logic supports the statement? Furthermore, as the theme of Part One of this paper shows, a very small proportion of the people living in the United States were allowed to vote. What can be said about the other 80 or so percent who were without a political voice? Could the argument be made that they prefer more local government—especially when the local governments were often the enforcers of the oppressions they were subject to?

This whole passage is packed full of wonderment. One conclusion from his arguments is that "the people" are not much interested in government unless they need it—see his discussion on the war: '*It was engaged, too, on a course of measures which had for their object the protection of everything that could be desirable to the people at large*'—the federal government was favored because the very life of the nation depended on it. Afterwards, they were more interested in local affairs. So a strong conclusion can be made from his arguments that when people are most endangered or most oppressed—the general population in times of war, and oppressed people such as Africans and descendants of Africans and poor white people in both war and peace—they are more likely to favor a strong federal government. Remove the oppression or danger and they are more concerned with local affairs, road repair, water supplies, building civic centers, etc. etc.

Madison's arguments here can lead to the conclusion that it is not whether people prefer a strong or weak federal government, it is which element of government can best serve me at this time or with the concerns that I have. This is consistent with his argument in *Federalist Paper Number 45* that "the public good, the real welfare of the great body of the people is the supreme object to be pursued."

This completes my review and commentary on the Federalist Papers and related documents. The rest of this study covers a variety of topics on modern day issues of governance and citizenship.

FREEDOM AND RESPONSIBILITIES

All of our founding documents hold conflicting goals—liberty / the pursuit of happiness; establish justice, domestic tranquility / blessings of liberty; liberty / justice.

What if you throw a dead cat on your neighbor's lawn as an expression of liberty, in the process destroy a part of the neighbor's right to justice, pursuit of happiness, not to mention domestic tranquility.

This case is an easy call. But what about flying a confederate flag in your yard? You have the liberty to do this. Do you have to consider your neighbor's feeling of happiness, tranquility, in or this case, creating a feeling of fear in the neighbor?

Viktor Frankl, a holocaust survivor, has an answer, He wrote in "Man's Search for Meaning," that the United States needs a Statue of Responsibility as well as a Statue of Liberty.

Viktor Frankl once recommended that the Statue of Liberty on the East Coast of the United States be complemented by a Statue of Responsibility on the West Coast:

"Freedom, however, is not the last word. Freedom is only part of the story and half of the truth. Freedom is but the negative aspect of the whole phenomenon whose positive aspect is responsibleness. In fact, freedom is in danger of degenerating into mere arbitrariness unless it is lived in terms of responsibleness. That is why I recommend that the Statue of Liberty on the East Coast be supplemented by a Statue of Responsibility on the West Coast." *Viktor Frankl*

We are in constant struggle in how to balance liberty and responsibility. In our modern world, with increasing populations, increasing wealth, and increasing economic activity, our actions more and more affect others. Sometimes other individuals, but more often whole populations—locally, nationally, and globally. This pushes us more toward the responsibility end and away from liberty and doing what we please. Destroying or emasculating the EPA will not make the challenge of having clean air, clean water, and lowering carbon dioxide in the air go away. It may increase our individual liberties—maybe lowering our taxes in the short run.

Responsibility extends to other citizens and groups of citizens. At one level of responsibility, we help clean up public places after we have used them, keep our grass mowed and weeds pulled partly because we feel responsible to our neighborhood. But as a nation, this requirement for responsibility goes much further. We should all be concerned with how our fellow citizens are doing in inner cities and racialized ghettos. What should we know about reservation conditions for our Indigenous Peoples? What should we as a nation be doing about the rapid changes in our economy that leave almost state-wide poverty? How should we react to all the rapid changes in our concepts of sexual orientation and gender identity? **The public good, the real welfare of the great body of people, is the supreme object to be pursued.**

I prefer the concept of citizenship to that of patriotism. Citizenship relates to responsibility to others. Humans living first in tribes and growing to larger organizations for connection took individual responsibility to see that the welfare others in the group was tended to. [There are, of course, many notable exceptions to this—feudalism, Russian communism, etc.] Citizenship in its ideal expression means that you have concerns for not only those close to you, but those that may be left out of access to the benefits of the larger society.

PUBLIC SCHOOLS

One of the most important institutions in the US is public schools. Our governments pay for public education, presumably because it is in the nation's best interest to have an educated population so that they have the knowledge to participate in democracy and have education and skills that will enable each person or family to make a living and contribute to the larger society. *John Stewart Mill*, cited earlier says that an educated population is essential for a thriving democracy.

We have public education, but what you get from it depends on where you live. A large part of financial support comes from property taxes and the receipts from these taxes vary enormously depending on the jurisdiction. So children of rich parents get good schools—children of poor parents, well——. If the state or county taxes at a level to support public schools that will enable kids to be superior students, the kids going there are lucky. For many, concern for public schools goes no further than, what is it doing for my kid? We don't want property taxes collected in our jurisdiction to be spent on schools in another jurisdiction.

And who controls public schools? Local school boards—of course. With federal support, local boards do have some requirements the schools must adhere to.

I question why we presume—and have for generations—that a local school board is the best governing body for a school. Could this also explain some of the vast differences in student accomplishments among the nation's public schools? It is in the interest of us as a nation that we have an educated citizenry. Why not have national standards and responsibilities for the nation's education?

As a nation, there must be some core set of knowledge and accomplishments that each of our kids should be expected to achieve by high school graduation. An exception is that some have challenges that prevent them from doing this.

Rather than local school boards, I am thinking about some of the ways knowledge is transmitted to citizens that participate in US Department of Agriculture programs. The way these work, is that extension agents for the Department are placed in many rural counties throughout the country. These provide many different services to citizens—good farming practices, knowledge of finances, various loan programs, household and family information, etc. Why couldn't something similar be set up for public schools? It would be available to all public schools in the country. Best education practices, textbooks for each learning level, teaching methods, teaching skills, etc. would be transmitted throughout the country. The goal would be that a kid has an equal chance of getting an adequate high school education no matter what part of the country she or he lives in. Remember, public schools are to educate the general population. They are not for indoctrinating the kids with certain belief systems. And they are not just for "our kids" but for all hundreds of thousands of kids in our public schools.

The idea that local parents and school boards know best is simply an assertion—not supported by any research that I know of. Of course, there is general opposition to federal standards and requirements in the wake of "no child left behind," and "common core." I think there was resistance was not in the concept of national expectations, but in their implementation.

This, of course, gets into beliefs, values, political preferences, etc. Local and State people want the freedom to educate children in certain ways—to have religious and political beliefs and values when they grow up.

HOW ARE WE DOING?

There is no way that government can serve all the interests of every citizen. We are a multiplicity of income levels, gender orientation and gender identity, ethnic group, religious preferences and on and on. So how is the government to be faithful to **the public good, the real welfare of the great body of people, is the supreme object to be pursued, and that no form of government whatever has any other value than as it may be fitted for the attainment of this object?**" *Madison, Federalist Paper Number 45.*

His reference to **the great body of people,** says to me that he is concerned with not only the 20 percent of the adult population that was allowed to vote, but also the 80 or so percent that was not allowed to vote—women, indentured servants, African and descendants of Africans held captives and consigned to forced labor, Indigenous People, non-Europeans, non-Christians, and others. (see Part One)

For those enfranchised to vote, the Constitution does well in providing for their needs. These are generally to have enough military power to dissuade other countries from invading us and interfere with international shipping, establishing diplomatic relations so that commerce, peaceful resolutions of conflicts can be done, establishing a unified monetary system, standardizing weights and measures, provide for systems to resolve differences and conflicts between states, etc. Although neither the Constitution, nor any statute that I am aware of requires that the US be a capitalist nation, property ownership was required in order to have a voice in the government.

Earlier, I speculated on what the 80 percent of the US residents would have looked to the Federal Government to provide. In modern times, as our society has grown and changed, our nation has expanded concepts of basic features the government should either provide or act to protect these needs. Franklin Roosevelt visualized a modern version of what these hopes and dreams could look like. This is the topic of the next section.

NEEDED CHANGES TO CONSTITUTION AND NATIONAL LAW

There are various reasons for government to engage in programs and activities of a democratic society. One is that spending money on specific areas or industries or activities benefits us all, even though we do not directly receive public funds. Examples of this are education and health. It has long been recognized that an educated population benefits that whole nation. Similarly with health, the whole nation benefits from generally good health, conversely the nation is worse off when segments of the population suffer from poor health.

A second reason is one of humanity, empathy, concern for our fellow citizens. This reason makes us work toward adequacy of housing, health, nutrition for all—sometimes without the expectation that there will be any national benefit in terms of economic growth or income distribution. We generally do not accept that some citizens live in unsafe, unhealthy, conditions.

The Federalist Papers contain many references to "the common good." What did they mean? Did it guide the writers of the Constitution? More importantly, how does it affect decision-making today? "The common good is a neglected topic in our politics. It is not identical to market forces, or to legal rules that maximize individual autonomy. It is the result of prudent public and private choices that strengthen community—the seedbed of human flourishing—and ensure the weak are valued and protected. The idea of the common good emerged from religious sources, but provides a broad, political common ground." *Gerson, p. A19*

Such concerns were not incorporated into our constitution. Over the centuries governments have committed—then withdrawn from these concerns, then committed again as new administrations and new expectations from the population have arisen. Franklin Roosevelt was concerned about this rise and withdrawal of concerns for basic welfare. So he proposed doing something about it.

"In an address known as the Four Freedoms speech (technically the **1941 State of the Union address**), Franklin Roosevelt proposed four fundamental freedoms that people "everywhere in the world" ought to enjoy:

1. Freedom of speech
2. Freedom of worship
3. Freedom from want
4. Freedom from fear

In the second half of the speech, he lists the benefits of democracy, which include economic opportunity, employment, social security, and the promise of "adequate health care". The first two freedoms, of speech and religion, are protected by the First Amendment in the United States Constitution. His inclusion of the latter two freedoms went beyond the traditional Constitutional values protected by the U.S.

Bill of Rights. Roosevelt endorsed a broader human right to economic security and anticipated what would become known decades later as the 'human security' paradigm in social science and economic development."
Roosevelt, Franklin D., Four Freedoms

This has formed the basis for expanding government to provide more of the needs of the people who were left out in the drafting and ratification of the Constitution.

Roosevelt went further in his 1944 State of the Union address where he proposed a Second Bill of Rights.

"The **Second Bill of Rights** is a list of rights that was proposed by United States President Franklin D. Roosevelt during his State of the Union Address on Tuesday, January 11, 1944. In his address, Roosevelt suggested that the nation had come to recognize and should now implement, a second "bill of rights." Roosevelt's argument was that the "political rights" guaranteed by the US Constitution and the Bill of Rights had "proved inadequate to assure us **equality in the pursuit of happiness**." His remedy was to declare an "economic bill of rights" to guarantee these specific rights:

- Employment, Food, clothing, and leisure with enough income to support them
- Farmers' rights to a fair income
- Freedom from unfair competition and monopolies
- Housing
- Medical care
- Social security
- Education

Roosevelt stated that having such rights would guarantee American security, and that the US's place in the world depended upon how far the rights had been carried into practice.

"During Roosevelt's January 11, 1944 message to the US Congress on the State of the Union, he said the following:

It is our duty now to begin to lay the plans and determine the strategy for the winning of a lasting peace and the establishment of an American standard of living higher than ever before known. We cannot be content, no matter how high that general standard of living may be, if some fraction of our people—whether it be one-third or one-fifth or one-tenth—is ill-fed, ill-clothed, ill-housed, and insecure.

This Republic had its beginning, and grew to its present strength, under the protection of certain inalienable political rights—among them the right of free speech, free press, free worship, trial by jury, freedom from unreasonable searches and seizures. They were our rights to life and liberty.

As our nation has grown in size and stature, however—as our industrial economy expanded—these political rights proved inadequate to assure us **equality in the pursuit of happiness.**

We have come to a clear realization of the fact that **true individual freedom cannot exist without economic security and independence.** "Necessitous men are not free men." People who are hungry and out of a job are the stuff of which dictatorships are made.

In our day these economic truths have become accepted as self-evident. We have accepted, so to speak, a second Bill of Rights under which a new basis of security and prosperity can be established for all—regardless of station, race, or creed.

Among these are:

- The right to a useful and remunerative job in the industries or shops or farms or mines of the nation;
- The right to earn enough to provide adequate food and clothing and recreation;
- The right of every farmer to raise and sell his products at a return which will give him and his family a decent living;

- The right of every businessman, large and small, to trade in an atmosphere of freedom from unfair competition and domination by monopolies at home or abroad;
- The right of every family to a decent home;
- The right to adequate medical care and the opportunity to achieve and enjoy good health;
- The right to adequate protection from the economic fears of old age, sickness, accident, and unemployment;
- The right to a good education.

All of these rights spell security. And after this war is won we must be prepared to move forward, in the implementation of these rights, to new goals of human happiness and well-being.

America's own rightful place in the world depends in large part upon how fully these and similar rights have been carried into practice for all our citizens. For unless there is security here at home there cannot be lasting peace in the world."

Roosevelt saw the Economic Bill of Rights as something that would, at least initially, be implemented by legislation, but that did not exclude either the US Supreme Court's development of constitutional jurisprudence or amendments to the US Constitution. Roosevelt's model assumed that federal government would take the lead, but that did not prevent states improving their own legislative or constitutional framework beyond the federal minimum. Much of the groundwork had been laid before and during the New Deal but left many of the Second Bill of Rights' aspirations incomplete. Internationally, the same economic and social rights were written into the Universal Declaration of Human Rights in 1948. *Roosevelt, Franklin D., The Economic Bill of Rights*

These proposals have formed the basis for many social changes since the Roosevelt Administration. As can be seen, many have been enacted into law, but no changes have been made to the Constitution to guarantee such rights. Executive orders and even laws can be changed by changes in the presidency and Congress. Only Constitutional changes will make them more permanent.

Roosevelt's list shows *the value and a danger* of incorporating these rights in the Constitution. After these several decades we see that the economic activities of the nation have changed drastically. We should not lock in support for selected economic activities. A specific right should not be made for farmers.

I wrote the following before I was aware (or perhaps had forgotten) that FDR had proposed a Second Bill of Rights. So you can check to see how my list below compares to his.

Many who read the following will immediately point out that this list is totally out of reach/impractical/wrong/etc. But we have to start somewhere. First set out the objective, then work toward that end. There have been many changes over the centuries in what we think is right and doable. We need to continue going in the right direction. You can say these are the thoughts of a dreamer. But there are many working to create a more just, compassionate world.

Let's start with my favorite quotation from the Federalist Papers found in *Number 45* by *James Madison*. "…It is too early for politicians to presume on our forgetting that **the public good, the real welfare of the great body of people, is the supreme object to be pursued, and that no form of government whatever has any other value than as it may be fitted for the attainment of this object.** Were the plan of the convention adverse to the public happiness, my voice would be, Reject the plan. Were the Union itself inconsistent with the public happiness, it would be Abolish the Union. **In like manner, as far as the sovereignty of the States cannot be reconciled to the happiness of the people, the voice of every good citizen must be, let the former be sacrificed to the latter.** How far the sacrifice is necessary has been shown. How far the unsacrificed residue will be endangered, is the question before us."

In keeping with Madison, the following should be done to accomplish "…**the public good, the real welfare of the great body of people, is the supreme object to be pursued…**"

Amendment One should be changed to prohibit anyone or entity who cannot vote for a candidate to spend money on her/his behalf. This includes PACs. Obviously, this precludes corporations, labor unions, etc. from spending money on political campaigns. Thus, a voter living in Iowa could spend money on the presidential election, but not on a US Senate candidate for Maryland. Without this provision we cannot fully enfranchise the voter and work toward the real welfare of the great body of people.

Amendment Two should be abolished. We no longer have State militias. And the Amendment as written has allowed for multiple interpretations so that at present we are forced to live in danger of violent and crazy people being allowed to carry and use firearms. Instead enact a federal law that possession of all firearms must be licensed so that only persons may be licensed that have been trained in the use and safety of the firearm they wish to purchase, including training in the safety of use of all firearms. Also, only persons having clean criminal records, not having been diagnosed with mental illnesses which may lead to violent behavior may be licensed. Firearms and other instruments that are designed for mass destruction would not be available for licensing to civilians.

Here is a question: Why do we not have a constitutional requirement that *candidates for US president be qualified for the job*? What we now have is democracy run amok. Trump is without question not qualified. No doubt it would be most difficult to come up with a set of qualifications besides the age and residency requirements we have now. An alternative to this is to constitute the Electoral College as it was described by *Hamilton* in *Federalist Paper Number 68* recorded above.

Under Hamilton's description of these Electors, they have a most solemn and difficult obligation—they must protect against "these most deadly adversaries of republican government [that] might naturally have been expected to make their approaches from more than one quarter, but **chiefly from the desire of foreign powers to gain an improper ascendant in our councils.**

I am skeptical that the Electoral College, either now, or as it was described by Hamilton would ever be able to, have the election, "made by men most capable of analyzing the qualities adapted to the station and acting under circumstances of deliberation, and to a judicious combination of all the reasons and inducements which were proper to govern their choice." "It was desirable that the sense of the people should operate in the choice of the person to whom so important a trust was to be confided. This end will be answered by committing the right of making it, not to any pre-established body, **but to men chosen by the people for the special purpose, and at the particular juncture.**" Even though Hamilton goes on to say that, "a small number of persons, selected by their fellow citizens from *the general mass*, will be most likely to possess the information and discernment requisite to such complicated investigations," *by the general mass*, he means white male property-owning Christians of European ancestry. *Alexander Hamilton* in *Federalist Paper Number 57* writes, "the aim of every political Constitution is, or ought to be, first to obtain for rulers men who possess most wisdom to discern, and most virtue to pursue, the common good of the society; and in the next place, to take the most effectual precautions for keeping them virtuous whilst they continue to hold their public trust." So now we know who he and the other founders considered having the most wisdom to discern, and most virtue to pursue, the common good of the society—white, property-owning men.

Issues of safety should be handled at the national level. Safe food and medicine, safe toys, safe household appliances, safe manufacturing and commercial equipment, safe water, clean air, should be handled at the national level—not dependent on the State or jurisdiction where a person lives. There can be an argument whether states can put requirements on more stringent than national standards.

Here is a modern case of how a State—and the EPA handled a public safety issue. **(on Flint Michigan) "Blame tainted nearly every arm of government, from Michigan's Republican governor, Rick Snyder and his Department of Environmental Quality, to the flat-footed E.P.A. to local elected officials." … "A church elder named Sarah Bailey soon chimed in, "It started with the decision that this community was inept and unable to govern itself," she said. "In 2011, Governor Snyder invoked a controversial state law and placed Flint under emergency management. A few years later, the city's emergency manager switched Flint's water source, a move that was driven, Bailey said, by the bottom line."…"She went on, "it took away our right to self-determination, self-governance, and democracy." *The New Yorker*, *January 23, 2017, Good Behavior*, *pp.46 – 55.*

Grants of incorporation, insurance and financial regulation should be done at the national level. Many or all of these are done at the state level. I see no justification for having multiple jurisdictions on these. In many cases, lobbyists have more power to get regulations to suit their interests if they only have to work at the state and local level.

Public schools would be funded to achieve a basic set of educational achievement across the nation. Basic curriculum is set at the federal level rather than states. Local school boards would have much less control over curricula, textbooks, etc. Education is so important to the long term welfare of the nation, that there should be a **constitutional guarantee** that every child will have access to an education that allows them to achieve a certain level of accomplishment. This would place it in the level of importance that federal expenditures would have to be made to achieve the goal. It would not be subject to the priorities of Congress and the Administration.

Justice at each jurisdiction should be standardized nationally. A US citizen should expect equal legal protection, bonding requirements, punishment etc. regardless of the part of the country he or she is being tried in. Issues of justice should be handled at the national level. These are universal values and a person should not be deprived of what others have just because they live in another place. No doubt it is not always clear whether some issues contain elements of justice. The right to vote is a most important justice issue and should be defined and enforced at the national level.

Government *health insurance* should be based on need. A person living with little income should receive free medical service. At the other extreme a billionaire has no need of government assistance to pay medical bills. Those in between would receive support based on income level. Medical facilities and personnel should be accessible in all parts of the country. Federal support should be provided where needed to assure this.

Everyone should be able to live in a *safe home and community.* The home should have basic features, such as adequate space, HVAC (where needed), safe water and working disposal systems. There should be absolute prohibition of any entity (from government to community organizations) restricting who can live in a community based on ethnicity, appearances or living styles. Federal support and enforcement should be provided where needed to assure this.

Everyone should have access to a *healthy adequate diet.* Federal support should be provided where needed to assure this.

Governments should not be involved with *how adults choose to relate to each other* in loving arrangements and living arrangements and should not discriminate based on the chosen arrangements.

Governments should not restrict how individuals identify themselves and should not discriminate based on chosen identities.

Appointments to the *Supreme Court should be limited* to 20 years—maybe 10 or 15. After this term, the judge could resume her/his duties as a federal judge inferior to the Supreme Court. This would discourage the current practice of nominating very young judges so that they can serve a very long time and continue the policies of the president who nominated them.

Voting eligibility in the US should not depend on where you live. Qualifications for voting should be solely done at the federal level. In the past few years, a number of states have put in place or attempted to put in place restrictions on voting that make it harder for young people, and some ethnic groups and in some cases, low-income people, to vote.

Adults that are not dependent on others should receive a **living wage**. This will vary, of course, on geographic location.

Finally, I will make a radical proposal. Recall again, Madison's words"…**the public good, the real welfare of the great body of people, is the supreme object to be pursued…**"

The Founders—those that had the right to vote—first established the United States as a confederacy, thinking that this was the best way to achieve "the public good." After about a decade they decided that a stronger federal government best achieved "the public good." So I presume that if Madison were still with us, he would encourage us to choose the form(s) of government that now advances the public good. Insisting on strict national boundaries to restrict the movement and living choices of people is definitely not achieving "the public good" for many people—US citizens and non-US citizens—living here.

So I believe that we should establish systems where persons living in any part of North and Central America can *move across borders* with minor restrictions, work in any of these countries, and pay into whatever social security system of the country they are working in and receive some benefit for having contributed to this system. For most of the past 500 years these borders have been porous with people and businesses moving back and forth largely to the benefit both of the people and countries. (Migrations across this area occurred for millennia, of course, before the coming of Europeans.) Why not codify it instead of the atrocious system we have right now? For voting, to be eligible, each person would have to declare citizenship in only one jurisdiction and live in that jurisdiction for some prescribed period of time. But for most of life's choices, we would benefit from way fewer restrictions on where people choose to live and work.

Epilogue

The Founders in getting the proposed Constitution to a point of ratification were of two minds. One that the States should retain most of the power, as was the case in the Articles of Confederation. The other, they were creating a new democracy with a republican form of government that would embrace all men and provide for the welfare of the great body of people. The Federalist Society by emphasizing the states' rights arguments of the Federalist Papers misleads readers as to their full content.

The debates at the constitutional convention and in the aftermath to promote ratification was between two groups; one wanting to stay close to the Articles of Confederation, and the other pushing for a more powerful federal government which could protect and enhance the positions of property owners. A third point of view (or maybe fourth and fifth, etc.) which was not represented at the convention was protection and enhancement of the lives of those without property, captive Africans and African descendants, indentured persons, women, and Indigenous Peoples. And even though the First Amendment calls for religious freedom, many state constitutions at the time placed restrictions on participating in voting and holding office based on religion.

The Constitution is a "hallowed" document. I hesitate to use this word, but can't think of a replacement. What I mean is that it is much more than a legal document. It called forth a new nation. It takes on a place of honor in human history. It is to be interpreted as a whole—not parsing words or phrases to wring out an interpretation that an advocate is seeking, such as might be done with a strictly legal document.

The nation has been on a tortuous path to correct some of the omissions in the Constitution to make our country more a nation of the people, by the people, and for the people. Notable are the thirteenth, fourteenth, fifteenth, and nineteenth amendments, elements of the New Deal, Supreme Court rulings on school desegregation, and the Voting Rights Act.

Notes

All bolding in this document is added to the original to highlight the relevant parts.

References

Primary Reference

Federalist Papers as recorded in Great Books of the Western World, Volume 43, <u>American State Papers, The Federalist, J. S. Mill</u>, Robert Maynard Hutchings, editor-in-chief, The University of Chicago, by Encyclopedia Britannica, 1952. Citations in the text identify individual papers.

Additional References

Batkins, *Sam*, <u>ABA Retains Little Objectivity in Nomination Process,</u> Center for Individual Freedom. August 12, 2004

Baum, *Lawrence and Devins, Neal,* <u>The Law, Lawyers, and the Court,</u> <u>Federalist Court,</u> Jurisprudence, Slate, January 31, 2017

Beard, Charles, <u>An Economic Interpretation of the Constitution of the United States</u>, New York, Macmillan, 1935 (as reproduced in Zinn)

Center for Individual Freedom, (CFIF) <u>Confirmation Watch</u>, undated

Dunbar-Ortiz, Roxanne. <u>An Indigenous Peoples' History of the United States,</u> ISBN 978-0-8070-5783-4 (paperback) Boston: Beacon Press, 2014

The Federalist Society, <u>Our Purpose</u>, and <u>Background</u> from The Federalist Society web page, September 2017

The Federalist Society ABA Ratings of Judicial Nominees". ABA Watch, July 1996 as an example.

Fletcher, Michael A., What the Federalist Society Stands For; Group Is Haven for Conservative Thought, The Washington Post, Washington, D.C. 29 July 29, 2005, p. A.21.

The General Court of the Commonwealth of Massachusetts, Resolves Passed at Their Session, CHAP. VI. Resolve regulating the choice of Electors of President and Vice President of the United States. June 15th, 1820.

Foster, Roger, Commentaries on the Constitution of the United States Historical and Juridical With Observations Upon the Ordinary Provisions of State Constitutions and a Comparison With the Constitutions of Other Countries, Volume I. Boston, The Boston Book Company, 1895.

Gerson, Michael, The religious right's new direction, The Washington Post, October 17, 2017

History.com Staff, January 07, 1789: First U. S. Presidential Election, 2009

History.com Staff, posted on the internet, September 2017

Hoffert, Robert W, Federalist Papers, Encyclopedia of Political Theory, February 2012

Hollis-Brusky, Amanda, Ideas with Consequences: The Federalist Society and the Conservative Counterrevolution. Oxford University Press, ISBN 9780199385539.2006 (2015).

Jilani, Zaid, For Most of Its History, the NRA Actually Backed Sensible Gun Regulation, Progressive Change, Campaign Committee, Boldprogressives.com, Retrieved 20 September2015.

Kaminski, John, A Necessary Evil?: Slavery and the Debate Over the Constitution, Madison House. ISBN 978-0-945612-33-9.1995

Ketcham, Ralph, ed., The Anti-Federalist Papers and the Constitutional Convention Debates, The Clashes and the Compromises That Gave

Birth to Our Form Of Government, Penguin Books Ltd., Registered Offices, Harmondsworth, Middlesex, England, 1986.

Labunski, Richard E., James Madison and the Struggle for the Bill of Rights, New York, Oxford University Press, ISNB-13: 978-0-19-518105-0, ISNB-10: 0-19518805-0, 2006, pp. 82-83.

Legislature of New York, Draft of a Resolution for the Legislature of New York for the Amendment of the Constitution of the United States, January 29, 1802

Lepore, Jill, The History Test, The New Yorker, March 27, 2017, p. 66 ff.

Lott, John R., Pulling Rank, The New York Times, Opinion, January 25, 2006

Madison, James, Letter to George Hay, Founders Online, August 23, 1823

McCarthy, Devin, How the Electoral College Became Winner-Take-All, FairVote, (an on-line resource) Posted August 21, 2012

McCarthy, Devin, Why James Madison Wanted to Change the Way We Vote For President, FairVote, (an on-line resource) Posted June 18, 2012

Mill, John Stuart. On Liberty, Representative Government, Utilitarianism, reproduced in, Great Books of the Western World, Volume 43, American State Papers, The Federalist, J. S. Mill, Robert Maynard Hutchings, editor-in-chief, The University of Chicago, by Encyclopedia Britannica, 1952

Morris, Irwin L. The American Presidency: An Analytical Approach. Cambridge University Press. *ISBN 978-1-139-49162-4. OCLC 607985767.* 2010, p. 67

Nash, Darrel A, A Perspective on How Our Government Was Built, And Some Needed Changes, Rose Dog Books, 585 Alpha Drive, Suite 103, Pittsburg PA 15238, ISBN 978-1-4809-7915-4, 2018

Roosevelt, Franklin D., Four Freedoms, *references include: FDR, "The Four Freedoms, Speech Text.* Wikipedia *Voicesofdemocracy.umd.edu. 1941-01-06. Retrieved 2014-08-14*

Roosevelt, Franklin D., <u>The Economic Bill of Rights,</u> <u>State of the Union</u> <u>Message to Congress</u>. American Heritage Center. Retrieved 10 November 2011

Schjonberg, Mary Frances, <u>General Convention renounces Doctrine of</u> <u>Discovery</u>, Episcopal Life Online, August 27, 2009.

Stewart, David O. <u>The Summer of 1787</u>. New York: Simon & Schuster. <u>ISBN</u> <u>978-0-7432-8692-3,</u> 2007

Stillman,Sarah, <u>Good Behavior</u>, The New Yorker, Condi Nast, 1 World Trade Center, New York NY 10007, January *23, 2017, pp. 46 – 55.*

Supreme Court of the United States, <u>Ray v. Blair</u>, No. 649, Argued: March 31, 1952, Decided April 15, 1952

United Nations Economic and Social Council, <u>Doctrine of Discovery,</u> <u>HR/5088</u>, May 8, 2012, Retrieved November 21, 2013.

UUA Website <u>Doctrine of Discovery and Rights of Indigenous Peoples,</u> UUA General Assembly 2012

Van Farowe, Roxanne, <u>Synod 2016 Rejects Doctrine of Discovery as</u> <u>Heresy,</u> Christian Reformed Church, June 17, 2016

Waldman, Michael, <u>The Second Amendment</u>, A biography, Simon and Schuster paperbacks, ISBN 978-1-4767-4745-3 (pbk) 2014.

Weible, Diane, <u>delegates overwhelmingly approve resolution repudiating</u> <u>Doctrine of Discovery,</u> General Synod of the United Church of Christ, July 1, 2013

Wikipedia, <u>Gerrymandering in the United States</u>, cited August 2017

Zinn Howard, <u>A People's History of the United States</u>, by New American Library, a Division of Penguin Putnam, Inc., HarperCollins Publishers, New York, New York 10022, ISNB 978-0*196558-6, 2003

Appendix

Excerpts from state Constitutions around the time of ratification of the US Constitution

Connecticut: All persons who have been, or shall hereafter, previous to the ratification of this Constitution, be admitted freeman, according to the existing laws of this State, shall be electors.

Every white male citizen of the United States, who shall have gained a settlement in this state, attained the age of twenty-one years, and resided in the town in which he may offer himself to be admitted to the privilege of an elector, at least six months preceding, and have a freehold estate of the yearly value of seven dollars in this state; or having been enrolled in the militia, shall have performed military duty therein for the term of one year next preceding the time he shall offer himself for admission, or being liable thereto, shall have been, by authority of law, excused therefrom; or shall have paid a state tax within the year next preceding the time he shall present himself for such admission; and shall sustain a good moral character; shall, on his taking such oath as may be prescribed by law, be an elector.

It being the duty of all men to worship the Supreme Being, the great Creator and Preserver of the Universe, and their right to render that worship, in the mode most consistent with the dictates of their consciences; no person shall by law be compelled to join or support, nor be classed with, or associated to, any congregation, church or religious association. But every person now belonging to such congregation, church, or religious association, shall remain a member thereof, until he shall have separated himself therefrom, in the manner hereinafter provided

Every white male citizen of the United States, who shall have attained the age of twenty-one years, who shall have resided in this state for a term of one year next preceding, and in the town in which he may offer himself to be admitted to the privileges of an elector, at least six months next preceding the time he may so offer himself, and shall sustain a good moral character, shall, on his taking such oath as may be prescribed by law, be an elector.

Delaware: All elections for governor, senators, representatives, sheriffs, and coroners, shall be held on the second Tuesday of November, and by ballot; and in such elections, every free white male citizens of the age of twenty-two years or upwards, having resided in the State one year next before the election, and the last month thereof, in the county where he offers to vote, and having within two years next before election paid a county tax, which shall have been assessed at least six months before the election, shall enjoy the right of being an elector, and every free white make citizen of the age of twenty-two years, having resided as aforesaid shall be entitled to vote without payment of any tax: *Provided* that [the provision continues saying this does not include military temporarily stationed in the state etc. etc.]

Georgia: We, therefore, the representatives of the people, from whom all power originates, and for whose benefit all government is intended, by virtue of the power delegated to us, do ordain and declare, and it IS hereby ordained and declared, that the following rules and regulations be adopted for the future government of this State:

The representatives shall be chosen out of the residents in each county, who shall have resided at least twelve months in this State, and three months in the county where they shall be elected; ... and they shall be of the Protestent religion, and of the age of twenty-one years, and shall be possessed in their own right of two hundred and fifty acres of land, or some property to the amount of two hundred and fifty pounds.

All male white inhabitants, of the age of twenty-one years, and possessed in his own right of ten pounds value, and liable to pay tax in this State, or being of any mechanic trade, and shall have been resident six months in this State, shall have a right to vote at all elections for representatives, or any other officers, herein agreed to be chosen by the people at large; and every person having a right to vote at any election shall vote by ballot personally.

Maryland: "That the house of delegates shall be chosen in the following manner: All freemen in this state, above twenty-one years of age, having a freehold therein of not less than fifty acres of land, and actually residing in the county in which he offers to vote; or having not less than forty pounds sterling property in the state, and having resided in the county in which he offers to vote, one whole year next preceding the elections, shall ... elect viva voce, by a majority of votes, four delegates for their respective counties, of the most wise sensible, and discreet of the people, residents in the state one whole year next preceding the election, above twenty-one years of age, and having in the state a freehold in lands or tenements, above the value of pounds sterling."

It is interesting what is said and not said in these documents. "Freemen" I am confident, means only men and excludes African and African descendants that are held captive and in forced labor. But could a free African or African descendant who possesses the assets specified above vote? Could Indigenous Peoples vote? Could non-Christians vote? This language doesn't say.

Massachusetts: "Every male person being twenty-one years of age, and resident in any particular town in this commonwealth, for the space of one year next preceding, having a freehold estate within the same town, of the annual income of three pounds, or any estate of the value of sixty pounds, shall have a right to vote in the choice of a representative or representatives for the said town.

The senate shall be the first branch of the legislature; and the senators shall be chosen in the following manner, viz: There shall be a meeting ... and at such meetings every **male** inhabitant of twenty-one year of age and upwards, having a freehold estate of the value of sixty pounds, shall have a right to give in his vote for the senators for the district of which he is an inhabitant.

[It seems the following also may be relevant to voting rights.] It is the right as well as the duty of all men in society, publicly and at stated seasons, to worship the Supreme Being, the great Creator and Preserver of the universe. And no subject shall be hurt, molested, or restrained, in his person, liberty, or estate, for worshipping God in the manner and season most agreeable to the dictates of his own conscience, or for his religious profession or sentiments, provided he doth not disturb the public peace or obstruct others in their religious worship.

And every denomination of Christians, demeaning themselves peaceably and as good subjects of the commonwealth, shall be equally under the protection of the law; and no subordination of any sect or denomination to another shall ever be established by law."

New Hampshire: "[Representatives, How Elected, Qualifications of.] Every member of the house of representatives shall be chosen by ballot; and, for two years, at least, next preceding his election shall have been an inhabitant of this state; shall be, at the time of his election, an inhabitant of the town, ward, place, or district he may be chosen to represent and shall cease to represent such town, ward, place, or district immediately on his ceasing to be qualified as aforesaid.

[Election of Senators.] The freeholders and other inhabitants of each district, qualified as in this Constitution is provided shall biennially give in their votes for a senator, at some meeting holden in the month of November."

I didn't find the precise wording for who is qualified to vote. As a side note—in 1776, New Hampshire was hoping that relationships with Great Britain would be restored and that they would continue to be a colony. Their (British) governor had departed out of fear of terrorists and so the legislature prepared a Constitution so that the functions of government could go on.

New York: "Every male citizen of the age of twenty-one years, who shall have been a citizen for ten days, and an inhabitant of this state one year next preceding any election, and for the last four months a resident of the county where he may offer his vote, shall be entitled to vote at such election in the election district of which he shall at the time be a resident, and not elsewhere, for all officers that now are or hereafter may be elected by the people; but such citizen shall have been, for thirty days next preceding the election, a resident of the district from which the officer is to be chosen for whom he offers his vote. **But no man of color**, unless he shall have been for three years a citizen of this state, and for one year next preceding any election shall have been seized and possessed of a freehold estate of the value of two hundred and fifty dollars, over and above all debts and incumbrances charged thereon, and shall have been actually rated and paid a tax thereon, shall be entitled to vote at such election. And no person of color shall be subject to direct taxation unless he shall be seized and possessed of such real estate as aforesaid." Bold added. The bar is raised for 'men of color.'

Pennsylvania: "In elections by the citizens, every freeman of the age of twenty-one years, having resided in the state two years next before the election, and within that time paid a state or county tax, which shall have been assessed at least six months before the election, shall enjoy the rights of an elector: Provided, that the sons of persons qualified as aforesaid, between the ages of twenty-one and twenty-two years, shall be entitled to vote, although they shall not have paid taxes."

North Carolina:

7. That all freemen of the age of twenty-one years, who have been inhabitants of any one county within the State twelve months immediately preceding the day of any election, and possessed of a freehold, within the same county, of fifty acres of land, for six months next before, and at the day of election, shall be entitled to vote for a member of the senate.

8. That all freemen of the age of twenty-one years, who have been inhabitants of any one county within the State twelve months immediately preceding the day of any election, and shall have paid public taxes, shall be entitled to vote for members of the house of commons, for the county in which he resides.

9. That all persons possessed of a freehold, in any town in this State, having a right of representation, and also all freemen, who have been inhabitants of any such town twelve months next before, and at the day of election, and shall have paid public taxes, shall be entitled to vote for a member to represent such town in the house of commons: provided, always, that this section shall not entitle any inhabitant of such town to vote for members of the house of commons for the county in which he may reside: nor any freeholder in such county, who resides without or beyond the limits of such town, to vote for a member of the said town

2. All free men of the age of twenty-one years (except as is hereinafter declared), who have been inhabitants of any one district within the State twelve months immediately preceding the day of any election, and possessed of a freehold within the same district of fifty acres of land, for six months next before and at the day of election, shall be entitled to vote for a member of the senate.

3. No free Negro, free mulatto, or free person of mixed blood, descended from Negro ancestors to the fourth generation inclusive

(though one ancestor of each generation may have been a white person) shall vote for members of the senate or house of commons.

The thirty-second section of the Constitution shall be amended to read as follows: No person who shall deny the being of God, or the truth of the Christian religion, or the divine authority of the Old or New Testament, or who shall hold religious principles incompatible with the freedom or safety of the State, shall be capable of holding any office or place of trust or profit in the civil department within this State.

Rhode Island and Providence Plantation: "Every male citizen of the United States, of the age of twenty- one years, who has had his residence and home in this state for one year, and in the town or city in which he may claim a right to vote, six months next preceding the time of voting, and who is really and truly possessed in his own right of real estate in such town or city of the value of one hundred and thirty -four dollars over and above all encumbrances, or which shall rent for seven dollars per annum over and above any rent reserved ...

Every male native citizen of the United States, of the age of twenty -one years, who has had his residence and home in this state two years, and in the town or city in which he may offer to vote, six months next preceding the time of voting, whose name is registered pursuant to the act calling the convention to frame this Constitution, or shall be registered in the office of the clerk of such town or city at least seven days before the time he shall offer to vote, and before the last day of December in the present year; and who has paid or shall pay a tax or taxes assessed upon his estate within this state ...

South Carolina: "Every free white man, of the age of twenty-one years, being a citizen of this State, and having resided therein previous to the day of election, and who hath a freehold of fifty acres of land or a town lot, of which he hath been legally seized and possessed at least six months before such election, or, not having such freehold or town lot, hath been a resident in the election district in which he offers to give his vote six months before the said election, and hath paid a tax the preceding year of three shillings sterling towards the support to this government, shall have a right to vote."

Virginia: "All freemen in this state, above twenty-one years of age, having a freehold therein of not less than fifty acres of land, and actually residing in the county in which he offers to vote; or having not less than forty pounds sterling property in the state."

The Constitution of Virginia June 29, 1776 1(1)

"That all men are by nature equally free and independent, and have certain inherent rights, of which, when they enter into a state of society, they cannot, by any compact, deprive or divest their posterity, namely, the enjoyment of life and liberty, with the means of acquiring and possessing property, and pursuing and obtaining happiness and safety ..."

"The right of suffrage in the election of members for both Houses shall remain as exercised at present; and each House shall choose its own Speaker, appoint its own officers, settle its own rules of proceeding, and direct writs of election, for the supplying intermediate vacancies."

Constitution of 1830

CONSTITUTION OF VIRGINIA.

14. Every white male citizen of the commonwealth, resident therein, aged twenty-one years and upwards, being qualified to exercise the right of suffrage according to the former constitution and laws; and every such citizen, being possessed, or whose tenant for years, at will or at sufferance, is possessed, of an estate of freehold in land of the value of twenty-five dollars, and so assessed to be if any assessment thereof be required by law; and every such citizen, being possessed, as tenant in common, joint tenant or parcener, of an interest in or share of land, and having an estate of freehold therein, such interest or share being of the value of twenty-five dollars, and so assessed to be if any assessment thereof be required by law; and every such citizen, being entitled to a reversion or vested remainder in fee, expectant on an estate for life or lives, in land of the value of fifty dollars, and so assessed to be if any assessment thereof be required by law; (each and every such citizen, unless his title shall have come to him by descent, devise, marriage or marriage-settlement, having been so possessed or entitled for six months;) and every such citizen, who shall own and be himself in actual occupation of a leasehold estate, with the evidence of title recorded two months before he shall offer to vote, of a term originally not less than five years, of the annual value

or rent of twenty dollars; and every such citizen, who for twelve months next preceding has been a housekeeper and head of a family within the county, city, town, borough or election district where he may offer to vote, and shall have been assessed with a part of the revenue of the commonwealth within the preceding year, and actually paid the same—and no other persons—shall be qualified to vote for members of the general assembly, in the county, city, town or borough, respectively, wherein such land shall lie, or such housekeeper and head of a family shall live. And in case of two or more tenants in common, joint tenants or parceners, in possession, reversion or remainder, having interest in land, the value whereof shall be insufficient to entitle them all to vote, they shall together have as many votes as the value of the land shall entitle them to: and the legislature shall by law provide the mode in which their vote or votes shall in such case be given: *Provided nevertheless*, That the right of suffrage shall not be exercised by any person of unsound mind, or who shall be a pauper, or a non-commissioned officer, soldier, seaman or marine, in the service of the United States, or by any person convicted of any infamous offence.

"Every white male citizen of the commonwealth, resident therein, and twenty-one years and upward, being qualified to exercise the right of suffrage according to the former Constitution and laws, and every such citizen being possessed, or whose tenant for year, at will or at sufferance, is possessed of an estate of freehold in land of the value of twenty-five dollars, and so assessed, to be if any assessment thereof by required by

169

law; and every such citizen, being possess, as tenant in common joint tenant or preserver, of an interest in an share of land, and having as estate of freehold therein, such interest or share being of the value of twenty-five dollars, and so assessed to be if any assessment thereof be required by law; (each and every citizen, unless his title have come to him by descent, devise, marriage, or marriage-settlement, having been so possessed or entitled for six months;) and every such citizen who shall own and be in actual occupation of a leasehold estate with the title recorded two months before he shall offer to vote, of a term originally not less than five years of the annual value of rent of twenty dollars; ...

Comment: this is the most twisted language I have ever seen.